endorsements
for *19*

Soooooo much work has gone into this book of yours! I'm taken back by the arrangement, effort, care and attention given to it. It's humble, thoughtful and gentle in style, yet it's strong and resolute in direction. Well done, Julian!

Dave Gilpin, Senior Pastor, Hope City Church

After being under Julian's leadership and guidance for two years, whilst leading a team of my own, I have benefitted tremendously from the close-up teaching and example of the principles in this book. It helped me be a better man, a better Christian and a better leader. Everything you are about to read truly comes from years of experience, practice, wisdom, and a thoroughly authentic example. Leadership truths last throughout generations, and *19* will stand amongst them.

Chris Meyer, Mission and Outreach Coordinator for The Grand, Clitheroe, UK

Leadership often begins with a simple act of saying, "Yes", and getting involved in God's adventure for your life. The journey of leadership always requires the encouragement of others, potential being spotted and then grown and developed. In this book we see Julian's heart and passion to inject much-needed encouragement into the next generation of leaders. *19* calls us to reflect on our stories and invites us to spark the leadership journey in others. Packed full of wisdom, insight and practical application, I hope this book will be read by young adults and those passionate about developing such leaders. Julian models the heart and character of leadership, showing faithfulness and commitment in raising other leaders up.

Pete Baker, National Director, PaisUK

What would I say to my nineteen-year-old self? That's the question that Julian wonderfully answers as he looks back on years of being found in spheres and positions of leadership. Julian approaches the question with candour, humour, creativity and wisdom. So, what would I say to the nineteen-year-old Paul Benger? I'd say, "Read a book called *19* . . . start there." I highly recommend this book to you, whatever your age and in whatever place you find yourself.

Paul Benger, Lead Pastor, IKON Church, UK

This book focuses on the central – but often overlooked – truth that leadership is a journey. When we commit to the journey, our leadership develops into a special gift, one worthy of serving others. This book will inspire young leaders on their own leadership journey to lead better and stay the path.

Andrew Cherrie, Lead Pastor, Home Church, St Albans, UK

Any investment into the potential of young leaders is a worthwhile investment! Julian demonstrates an ability to appreciate and apply Biblical wisdom, discerned through years of faithfully learning and growing in the heart of his local church. He writes clearly, articulately and persuasively. *19* is a book which will equip, inform and empower young leaders for the critical role of Christian leadership.

Steve Mawston, Pastor, Hillsong Brisbane

This well-written Christian leadership book flows from Julian's personal leadership journey. It is immensely practical and delightfully readable. However, don't let the title deceive you: this is not just for nineteen-year-old emerging leaders. It is for every leader who once was nineteen.

I've been in Christian leadership for nearly forty years, and I found *19* to be fresh, relevant and a wonderful stimulus to help me stay true to my personal leadership journey. I highly recommend it for both you and those you are helping to develop as leaders.

Stephen Matthew, Speaker, coach, author and Principal of the
Building Church Academy

I have known Julian for some time now and admire his zeal and zest for life. He has a unique way of injecting life into the situations in which he finds himself. Now he has achieved that through writing this book. Having written a good number of books myself I know how much work and effort is needed. This book is easy to read, covering complex issues in an uncomplicated way, allowing and encouraging self-assessment as you read. It addresses the challenges you will face as a leader and allow you to develop your style accordingly. I particularly enjoyed the chapter on 'Layers not Levels' – what a great thought, one that helps leaders shift in their approach to life as we lay down foundations as layers. I can thoroughly recommend this book! It's for everyone.

Dr. Scott Wilson. Founder of ICLM, President of Eurolead.net

One of the greatest gifts a leader can have is faithfulness. In the instant generation we live in, full of quick fixes and fast-paced changes, longevity is vastly overlooked and faithfulness is undervalued. Within the kingdom of God, we especially understand the role it has to play. In the parable of the talents, Jesus uses the phrase, "Well done, good and faithful servant". Not successful, not highly educated, not famous . . . faithful! Faithfulness is essential to strong leadership. With over twenty-five years of leadership experience, Julian Clark has already done far greater than many others, because he has led with faithfulness. This book is testament to that. *19* is the story of a faithful leader, who has embraced the challenges and joys of leadership for well over two decades. This book is packed full of great lessons, stories and examples that any leader can learn from. As a leader, I always want to learn from people with experience, not just education; people who can guide me on a path that they've actually walked themselves. The principles given in 19 are not just theory, but lessons that have been learned through real-life failures and success. The experiences shared in these pages and questions asked of the reader will help you to grow as a leader, whatever your current capacity.

Ben Dowding, Senior Pastor of Influence Church, UK

Julian delivers to us proven and tested leadership principles from the trenches of his own life. This book has the potential to be a powerful tool in the hands of anyone desiring to kickstart or reboot their leadership. I'm buying copies for my leaders!

Jonny Clarke, Lead Pastor, City Life Church, Sunderland

19

19

LEADERSHIP LESSONS I WOULD TELL MY YOUNGER SELF

JULIAN CLARK

This edition published in 2017 by Great Big Life Publishing
Empower Centre, 83-87 Kingston Road, Portsmouth, PO2 7DX, UK.

British Library Cataloguing in Publication Data. A catalogue record for this book is
available from the British Library

ISBN: 978-0-9957925-4-8
eBook: 978-0-9957925-5-5

contents

dedications

To my beautiful wife Kerina, for her continued encourage-ment, love and support for the past twenty-three years together.

To Kevin and Tina Hudson, who saw something in me and gave me that first leadership opportunity back in 1989.

To Ed and Hilary Grundy, just a wonderful, generous couple who looked after me like a son.

And to my three beautiful daughters, Lucy, Maisie and Grace. Thank you for encouraging your dad to stop talking about this and to actually 'get on with it'.

<u>th</u>ank yous

I want to say thank you to all those who have encouraged me on my leadership journey. Some will never know the influence they have had on my life. Through books I have read, through conferences attended and podcasts listened to. Thank you to Paul Scanlon, Andy Stanley, Bill Hybels, John C. Maxwell and Craig Groeschel – your leadership journeys have shaped mine.

To those who have supported this book through the kickstarter project, thank you.

Sharon Watterson, Grace Clark, Janice Coombes, Richard McGuinness, Denise Wiseman, Alvaro Fuenzalida, Phil and Rachel Thomson, Darren Neil, Lee Johnson, Joshua and Faith Barr, Sam Cotterill, Adam Blyde, Traff and Vanessa Street, Dave and Beccy Gibson, Evie Booth, Pauline Denham, Elizabeth Proud, Karen Thurlbeck, Vicky Hewish, Steve and Jo Dixon, John Crick, Gary Hosey, James Ross, Sarah Street, Benjamin Griffiths, Julie Christey-Barker, Rosie Laxton, Chris Meyer, Martin Jude, Julie Sutherland.

To Mum and Dad – thanks for the support and encouragement, for believing in me and celebrating me, for the great example of how to lead well through all different kinds of situations, for your consistent faith-filled walk with God. You have shaped the way I lead, not only in my role within Church but also with my family too.

<u>fo</u>rewords

Leadership is a tricky art.

Those are two loaded words! Tricky: not in the sense of deceit or crafty but that leadership requires skill and care because it is difficult. Leadership is difficult. We work with people who have their opinions, experience and skill set. We, too, as leaders come with the same paradigm. This is all thrown into the pot of organisational setting and must work.

But leadership is also an art. Max De Pree describes leadership as "jazz". Jazz involves intuition, skill, teamwork and flair. Jazz requires all the musicians to work together but move, ebb and flow as needed to create a sound people want to listen to.

Leadership, by definition, is always looking forward and

finding ways to create new opportunity. Leadership requires skill and thought. But most of all, leadership always stands on the shoulders of others. It means that this tricky art requires reflection and thought.

Julian Clark has written a book that goes back to the beginnings of leadership life, to the time where we were ready to learn, the time when each of us began our journey in leadership. When Julian asked me the question, "What would you tell your nineteen-year-old self, knowing what you know now", I was intrigued and captivated by the question. I have actually used (stolen) this idea and used it at leadership teachings and seminars. It is a great question and one that helps get to the heart of this tricky art of leadership.

This book is full of wisdom that can instruct and advise any leader at any time in their journey. The layout is concise and easy to follow, with personal reflection questions at the end of each chapter. Along with this, Julian has included answers to his insightful question from a number of seasoned leaders. He has tackled the issue of trait leadership (character) in a provocative but challenging way.

Any leader needs to constantly learn the art they have decided to work with. Leaders need all the help they can get. I have found reading to be one of the most positive and enlightening ways of doing this. Books never fail. They reveal, test, challenge and identify the change needed.

This is that kind of book, and it deserves a place on your reading table.

Yes, this leadership journey truly is a tricky art, but with people like Julian who are prepared to research, write and present good quality work, it all becomes easier. You may never have to ask that same question of your nineteen-year-old self because you learnt from the best! Thank you, Julian, for your book. Well done.

Dr. Scott Wilson. Founder, ICLM. President of Eurolead.net.

When I was nineteen, it was 1987, the greatest decade for music EVER! (Don't even argue, ha ha!). I was 'in between jobs', I sported a very cool 'mullet' hair style (don't judge me) and was starting out in leading a youth group at my church alongside my friends and under the leadership of my parents. We were opening our new church building and it was an exciting time to be a youth leader starting out in ministry.

I knew very little about leadership, I knew a little more about playing the piano and leading people in praise and worship, and I cared about my friends and contemporaries on the journey of faith we were exploring. I knew that I needed help, though. I needed resources – whether that was people who could inspire me and mentor me, tapes I could listen to, and books I could read.

One thing my mum always said to me was, "Remember, John, people are watching you. If you think it's okay to do that, then they will think it's okay for them. So be aware."

That was something I appreciated, but also slightly resented. Why me? Why did I have to be the example, just because I'm a Pastor's kid?

Of course, she was right (she often was), and I discovered the power of example cuts both ways, both positively and even in a negative way.

I didn't know much about leadership, but I did begin to realise the enormous power of example, and how the way we live doesn't have to be and can't be perfect, but we are called to model a life which 'stands out' in terms of our integrity and character. I didn't know this, but these were the first signs of an understanding of how leadership is influence and how this can be both positive and negative.

We can therefore all lead, because we can all learn to influence, and Julian's book is a call to be a positive influence on those around us and the wider world. As you will see through the pages of this book, leadership, like life, is a journey – a journey of discovery, of self-awareness, and learning, whether through our mistakes and failures, or seeming successes.

The key is to learn from the lessons and to apply the principles that others have picked up.

The rear view mirror is a powerful lens to look back on. Many would say hindsight is a powerful thing. Often we say that with a tinge of regret, "If only I'd known that".

This book is a very helpful handbook or travel guide to help us navigate our own path. Julian is honest and vulnerable as he lays bare some of the turning points on his journey that have forged his path. Julian's heart and passion is to add value and be a resource to you, whether you are starting on this path of leadership or you are further into the story. Having worked with Julian as a Pastor, and been his friend over many years, the truths he points to here have been 'road tested' in life and therefore can be applied with confidence.

I wish I had had this book in my hands when I was nineteen. I would have still made mistakes, I would have still learned my own lessons, but this guide would have given me assurance and confidence that I can use every experience to help me on the journey. Take this book and use it, I believe it will help the nineteen-year-olds and anyone wherever they are in life to lead well.

John Greenow, Lead Pastor, Xcel Church, County Durham

hello, this is me

Who am I to be writing a leadership book? No one special, just an ordinary bloke who found himself invited into the leadership journey as a young man and who has tried to keep walking it the best he can ever since.

What you're about to read is my journey. In some ways it's just a bunch of random thoughts and stories but they represent me and my learning. I have done my best to be honest, open and transparent, a little vulnerable at times, just so you get a feel for what leadership actually involves.

It can be difficult to give proper context to stories. Some of them come from what I lovingly call the 'University Years', when I lived as a Christian alongside continuing, at times, to live like I wasn't one.

In addition to those from the early leadership years, I will make mention of different experiences from throughout my leadership journey. All of which have been learned along the way as a team leader, learning mentor in schools, life coach, being a Congregational Pastor, and my current role as Executive Pastor in Xcel Church.

Add being a husband and father to three beautiful daughters, and there have been plenty of places to gain understanding about what it means to be the right kind of leader.

The book is in three sections: BEGINNING, MIDDLE and NOW. Don't let the numbering of chapters confuse you, even they represent the journey and the way everything we need to learn is connected.

There are some guest contributions from leaders in my world who have shared their own take on what they would tell their nineteen-year-old self.

My hope is that you will not only enjoy reading about my leadership journey but learn from it as well. To help with this there are some questions at the end of each chapter encouraging you to think, reflect and have your own moment of self-awareness. Stuff like, how is your leadership doing? How does this particular aspect of leadership play out for you? In what ways do you think you may need to change?

I've even left space for you to make some notes and some

actions too. The opportunities for you to learn something and maybe change something, that's really why I wrote this.

The way the book is set up may also provide opportunity for you to sit with your own team of leaders and read a chapter together and then reflect together.

A leadership definition

I was encouraged by someone about writing my own definition of leadership. Instead, my hope is that as you read you will discover the things which, in my opinion, are some of the key characteristics any leader should be focused on.

Whether you lead in a church, in business, at work or at home, I am confident all of what you are about to read can help you become a better leader.

Julian Clark

part one:
beginning

19.0 The Start

all leaders have to start s̲omewhere

Nineteen. This is the age I was when I was given my first leadership opportunity. It was late 1989. And feels like a lifetime ago. I had been a Christian (of sorts) for about three years. I knew little or nothing about being a leader. I probably thought I knew everything but, in all honesty, I knew nothing, and when I say nothing, I mean about being a leader and also about being a Christian.

Not exactly sure what Kevin and Tina Hudson, those in charge of the youth at the church, saw in a skinny, lanky, nineteen-year-old lad who hadn't been around very long. Even now, looking back, the question 'why did they ask me and not someone else' still runs through my mind. Why not choose someone with some sort of experience?

I had only been in the church for about six months. There were people who had already been involved and part of the church for years, as well as knowing the young people better than me.

Their answer was simple: *'We saw in you the potential to lead from "behind". This was important as too many leaders lead out of their own need to be seen, rather than a need to give.'* They definitely saw something in me I did not know was there.

In fact, when we get given our first opportunity the truth may be that why we have been given it is actually hard for the one who asked us to define; there is just a 'feeling' you are the right person for the role.

Now, more than twenty-five years on, I am thankful they gave me a go. All these years on, I'm now trying to articulate what I would say to someone who is nineteen and just like me back then, feels equally unprepared to step into the leadership arena for the first time. This is where the whole idea of the book comes into play – *'if I only knew then what I know now'.*

▍ What have I learned on the journey?

▌ How would I describe that journey?

▌ If any, what have been the golden moments?

▌ What have been those moments best forgotten?

▌ What should a new leader expect along the way?

I've been scribbling this stuff down for the past few years but I've just lacked the discipline to pull it all together. So here goes. My life as a leader.

I might ask the question, who do I think I am? Who am I to share my thoughts? An ordinary nineteen-year-old who, at the time, thought he was cool but most of all just said *'yes'*.

▌ I made myself available.

▌ I gave it a go.

▌ I stepped up to serve, wherever and whenever. *(I think during the past twenty-five plus years I have done most things)*.

▌ I have been around longer than most people.

▌ I will do what needs to be done.

▌ I have had a willingness to learn and keep learning.

My credentials for writing on this subject come from over

twenty-five years of leadership experience in a whole host of different roles, providing an ample amount of stories to share and plenty of positive and more awkward learning opportunities. Like all of us in some kind of leadership role, I am still learning but we all have to start somewhere. The adage 'use what you have, do what you can, start where you are' would be a great way to describe my attitude to life and leadership.

to my 19-year-old self:

" We can't learn anything if we are not willing to start. So here's to your journey. Say 'yes'. Give it a go. Enjoy it. Go for it. Use what little courage and knowledge you think you have to take that role on. Then, along the way take the time to think, reflect and, when appropriate, to be challenged to make some kind of response too. **"**

questions:

How old were you when you were given the opportunity to lead?

What do you think they saw in you?

19.1 Steps

leadership is a series of steps

It's not a destination, just a journey.

When I think of my first steps, they started more as a series of what I might consider 'hopeful' steps.

❚ I hoped I would get away with it.

❚ I hoped I wouldn't fall flat on my face.

❚ I hoped I wouldn't mess up.

❚ I hoped some kids would turn up.

❚ I hoped they would come back the following week.

❚ I hoped that some might actually learn something.

It took a boat load of trust. From those who asked me and then from me, in God and in my leaders. Of putting my very simple, unformed faith in God to use. All the normal emotions were there; I was scared and daunted by the prospect of it being me who was responsible for what was about to happen, to be the one out front, of having to talk and be a youth leader. In all honesty, when I reflect on the madness of it all, I did not have a clue what I was doing.

My first leadership opportunity was to be the leader of the church youth group. We called it JCs. I didn't pick the name. At least I don't think I did. And it wasn't named after me. More a play on 'Just Christians' or some similar kind of idea. It was 1989 for goodness' sake. There was cheese even back then, we just didn't know it was. We all thought it was cool.

Right at the beginning, taking those first steps on the leadership journey, there were three very important discoveries about leadership . . .

❚ Leadership steps take courage.

❚ Leadership steps take faith.

❚ Leadership steps take time.

Basically all three of these are code for lots of hard work and effort. As a nineteen-year-old these were not things I had ever considered before but they are massive.

To be a leader means being willing to take the steps. Steps which are not always easy. In fact, they will probably feel clunky and awkward at first. Be encouraged, everyone who learns to walk falls over, makes mistakes. The key is to just keep trying, learning and getting back up again. If those first ones feel tough, then I guarantee there will be equally as tough ones in the future and many tougher ones too. This is leadership.

We have to be willing to make a plan for the steps we are about to take. Don't just launch in without some thought, some kind of preparation. Think of the cost. John C. Maxwell talks about how leaders have to *give up to go up'*, to sacrifice, and I've experienced that quite often. The thing about steps is that once we have taken one and feel like we've mastered the art of taking them, something comes along to test our leadership in a different way and we find ourselves feeling stretched once again, stumbling along, falling, possibly even failing.

Been there. Done that. But it doesn't have to be the end.

I have messed up in every way possible when it comes to leadership. Others would be more qualified to tell you how. I certainly wasn't trying to deliberately get it wrong or upset people, I was just trying my best, taking a step.

The biggest test is often found in how we respond to the mistake; whether we learn and grow or, alternatively, feel leadership isn't really for us. We have to decide to be a leader who wants to improve, learn and to be making some kind of progress.

A key aspect in helping me take these steps in my various leadership roles since then has been to keep my walk with God right. Not always mastered this. However, I have discovered that if this is strong and healthy then everything else seems to be strong and healthy too. The opposite can also be true.

In those early days I was definitely more 'titled' as leader, than living with what would be considered those leadership essentials. Isn't that the journey though? If it were a destination, the messing up along the way would have had me give up long ago. God's belief in me is always greater than the belief I have in myself or that others may have in me. Where my sin has abounded, His grace has abounded so much more. I am thankful for this powerful truth. Without the confidence of this truth about the availability of God's grace there would have been times when the next step would not have happened.

to my 19-year-old self:

" Trust that those who asked you have seen something in you and, more than that, trust God's ability to create something with someone who is willing to start taking those tentative leadership steps. Keep time with God as a priority. Keep an eye on this as everything else is impacted by the health of this one relationship. *"*

questions:

How were your first steps?

How has keeping in step with God helped you with your steps as a leader?

part two: middle

leadership is about people

After keeping my trust in God strong, one other thing kept me going. People. I was at university in Sheffield at the time and the church I was part of wasn't large but it had a good bunch of young adults in it and we all shared the same passion for wanting to serve. As I have commented already, none of us really knew what we were doing but we had a willingness to give it a try. We would definitely succeed or fail together.

I am grateful that we had each other. For the sense of team and camaraderie. Even more than that, I was thankful for the friendships. We had fun. We had a laugh. We did life together. We supported one another, prayed for one another, encouraged each other. We fought for each other too.

As a group of friends we also had the investment from a couple in the church who not only encouraged us, but opened up their home to us, helped us in our thinking, prayed with us, and really believed in our ability to make a difference.

Their trust in us, a team of leadership newbies, was pretty amazing. I think I spent as much time with them as I did getting my university work completed (maybe more sometimes). Because of the way they were I have an immense sense of gratitude to the investment from the legends who are Kevin and Tina Hudson. They actually took a punt on a bunch of young leaders, and that right there is a challenge to all of us who lead now to always be doing the same.

Having the right kind of people around me kept me on the leadership journey. Despite my best efforts at times to sabotage my own leadership with some dubious lifestyle choices, which are best left unmentioned, having the right voices speaking into my life was invaluable.

I have definitely learned that the following is very true . . .

Leadership is about people:

❚ The people you lead.

▌ The people you lead with.

▌ The people who lead you.

The right leaders. The right team. The right friendships.

Leaders who were great at encouraging, empowering and releasing me but were also willing to deal with any awkward moments, and keep me accountable too.

Team who helped to carry the vision, worked as hard as me to make things happen, and have an attitude of 'shared responsibility'.

Friends who I could have a laugh with, be honest with, and, when I messed up, would stick by me. Friends in good times are amazing, but friends through hardship are even more precious. I was glad for friends like these.

From all three . . .

I was continually **challenged** to give things a go.

I was regularly **confronted** about those dubious lifestyle choices.

I was beginning to **change** into the person God needed me to be *and knew I could become.*

I was developing the **character** of a leader.

to my 19-year-old self:

" Never allow the 'in-charge' aspects of leading cause you to hurt those you lead. Don't abuse these key relationships as you journey in leadership. Appreciate your leaders and value the friends who are leading alongside you. **"**

questions:

Who are the people that you are thankful for?

Who are those who have challenged and confronted you, who have brought about good change in you and developed the right kind of leadership character in you?

19.2.1 Challenge

leadership means challenge

During those early days of leadership, it was all about being challenged.

Challenged to take massive steps into the unknown. To do new things. As I've mentioned before, I was scared, nervous, unsure and I have learned through the years that these feelings are alright and even after being a leader for another twenty-five years they are still as real. They show that you care.

First steps are the most challenging steps. Doing a whole bunch of stuff for the first time and not really knowing if it will even work. I had no one to look to as an example. Resource was harder to come by back then than it is today.

For the first time ever I had to lead a group of young people. *[Imagine a scared face]*

For the first time ever I was responsible for coming up with some sort of programme, some ideas, to be creative in my thinking, and it needed to be something which would keep the interest of a bunch of teenagers and *hopefully* they would even enjoy it.

For the first time ever I had to turn up and produce. It was on me. And my team. Although I'm fairly sure they were glad they weren't the leader and that the majority of the pressure was on me.

For the first time ever I had to listen to others critique what *was* produced. I had to learn to take this on the chin, accept both the good feedback and the harder comments too, to be ready to listen and then work at making any necessary changes.

For the first time ever I had to teach, in a relevant way, about Jesus, to pray with young people, and to think how Christian truths should be put across to a group of young people.

Maybe you can relate.

I was terrified.

But I loved it.

I was hooked.

My leadership journey had begun.

Leadership definitely means challenge.

▌ Without challenge we don't grow. *We stagnate.*

▌ Without challenge we don't learn. *We become outdated and old before our time.*

▌ Without challenge we don't discover what we can do.

▌ Without challenge we don't discover what we cannot do.

▌ Without challenge we don't make mistakes and mistakes are often the place where we learn the most. Or should be.

▌ Without challenge we don't progress. *We fall behind.*

▌ Without challenge we don't stay sharp. Instead we begin to settle, get easily bored, and become mediocre.

▌ Without challenge we don't fulfil our potential or at least we aren't being pushed to reach that potential. *We miss out on all that God has planned for us.*

to my 19-year-old self:

" To be a leader, get ready to embrace the challenges. It can be uncomfortable because of the stretch, but stretch is okay, in fact it's essential. Just stick in, feel the pain, keep stretching, keep stepping up, growth happens here and you can become the leader you have the potential to become and want to become. **"**

questions:

What challenge scares you the most?

What challenge has grown you the most as a leader?

19.2.2 Confrontation

leadership involves learning the hard way

This is hard to write about. Confrontation is rarely easy; let's be honest, it can be downright terrifying, whether you are the one being confronted or the one doing the confronting.

I remember very clearly a meeting I was called to where it quickly became apparent that the sole agenda was to discuss those dubious lifestyle choices I have already alluded to.

I was twenty-one. It was awkward. Actually it was extremely uncomfortable and I hated every moment.

It was all of these things for just one reason – my leaders were right.

The challenge of the right lifestyle choices is a big one. The argument of 'everyone else is behaving this way' doesn't wash for anyone who wants their leadership to really make a difference.

My university years were a mixed bag when I was learning this as I tried to live my 'spiritual' life and 'university' life as two separate ones. The conversation was all about reminding me that this ultimately cannot work.

Leaders cannot call those in their care to attain to a certain lifestyle which they may look like they are living yet in reality they are not. Let's call this what it is: hypocrisy and completely unfair.

Confrontation is not easy to take at the best of times but it is especially difficult when what you are being told about yourself is, in fact, the truth. Awkward.

Here's what I learned when being confronted at this time about my life and why it was important in regards to my leadership ...

❙ They spoke to me because they loved me. They believed

in me and wanted the best of God for me.

▌ They had a strong desire to protect my leadership credibility.

▌ They were wanting to make sure I didn't sabotage my God-given destiny for what were just selfish behaviours as it could potentially sabotage the God-given destiny of those I led, too.

▌ They had a bigger view and saw the dangers I had become blinded to. They had an eye on my future, while mine was just on what was happening in the moment.

▌ They were not concerned about my leadership ability, what I could do. This was about creating the opportunity for me to refocus in regards to how I lived. This was about who I could become.

The result was me stepping down from my leadership role for a time. In responding well it made it easier for them to bring me back on team later in the year.

I now have an appreciation for the courage it took for them to initiate this conversation even though they knew it would not be easy. It's equally as tough to be the leader now, doing the confronting.

If you truly love those you lead then confrontation is unavoidable. After all, whether we like it or not it's usually through the tougher conversations when we grow. Confrontation from a good leader is the stretch we so often require in preparation for the next phase of our life as a leader. When delivered from a place of love and care for the individual concerned, it's an incredibly powerful leadership quality.

I'm not sure I want to think about where I would be now if that 'chat' hadn't happened. It saved me from my immature self and undoubtedly contributed to make me a better leader. Added, of course, to all the other similar chats which have happened since. *[I'll come back to this later in the book].*

to my 19-year-old self:

" Like it or not, be ready for some confronting of your leadership. No one goes looking for it but there will be times of awkwardness. Hopefully they will come from leaders who believe in you, care for you and don't want you to damage the future you have as a leader, wherever that might end up being in life. **"**

questions:

What's your experience of confrontation?

How has it helped you to grow as a leader?

19.2.3 Change

leadership always means you are willing to change

At nineteen you feel pretty invincible. The world needs to be ready for the awesomeness that is you.

As a nineteen-year-old stepping into leadership for the first time I can, with almost absolute certainty, know that the need for me to change was not very high on my agenda. However, it would have definitely been necessary somewhere in my make-up.

I am not perfect now; I'm 100 per cent sure I wasn't back then.

▌ I was probably a little precocious. Sorry but most of us are in our teenage years.

▌ I probably thought that no one could tell me anything. What do those old people know anyway?

▌ I probably had the opinion that I knew what I was doing.

▌ I probably felt like 'this is it', I have made it. I am on the way to fame.

Without a doubt my people skills were not yet honed. I upset people when I said things. As I've said before, there were times when my life and my leadership didn't marry up.

Quietly and carefully those around me changed me. Sometimes in a more deliberate manner, other times less obviously. There was no formal leadership development programme when I started, it was much more about learning as you go, change as you go.

If you won't embrace change, you won't be staying as a leader for very long.

How has understanding the idea of change helped me?

Here is what I have learned.

CHANGE . . .

brings **C**larity

can be **H**ard

helps develop the right **A**ttitude

should be **N**ormal

Grows you

creates **E**nergy

Clarity

Like it or not change means being honest, open and transparent about the current level of my own leadership skills. Followed by being willing to clearly identify the areas that need to be improved and actually working on improving them.

Hard

Seems obvious to say, but it's never easy admitting that you need to change, but if I hadn't then I would not have got any better as a leader. Just because it's hard doesn't mean I shouldn't attempt it. Sometimes we just have to battle our way through some stuff as it will help us to become better.

Attitude

Developing the right attitude is essential and the right

kind of change can help in this process. To not work on my attitude would have been the quickest way to disqualify myself from any leadership role.

Normal

As Giuseppe Tomase di Lampedusa in his novel *The Leopard* wrote, 'If we want things to stay the same, things will have to change.' Like it or not, change has to become a normal part of our leadership. For ourselves and for those we lead.

Growth

If I want to grow then I need the uncomfortableness which change often brings, some stretch and challenge as talked about in a previous chapter, all working to make me more effective as a leader.

Energy

A change in the programme, some new ideas, a different leader, new team members, a shift of focus – all of these can bring fresh energy, passion and life to something that has maybe gone stale.

Everything we do is an opportunity to learn and therefore an opportunity to change. We must always be open to the need for change and embrace it rather than fight it. Change may not be inevitable but it is necessary. *[Or should that be change may not be necessary but it is always inevitable?]*

To see the need for change is one thing: in my head it makes perfect sense; I know it's right. Far off change sounds wonderful. The transition, however, from knowing in my head to it being in my heart, that journey can just take a little longer.

to my 19-year-old self:

" If you are up for this leadership stuff then get ready for the ride and adventure of your life. You will love it and hate it, maybe both at the same time, but one thing is for sure: you won't be the same when you come out the other side. You will be changed and that's a good thing. Why not help the process and identify some changes you know need to be made. **"**

questions:

How have you changed as a leader?

In what ways has that change been difficult but worth it in the end?

what would you tell your 19-year-old self about leadership?

andrew cherrie

lead pastor of Home Church, St Albans, UK

I would tell myself to keep things simple. There's a great acronym that's become my mantra over the years and this is what I'd share with my nineteen-year-old self – KISS: Keep It Simple Stupid. I'd explain that as leadership develops and opportunities appear, life has the danger of becoming so complex it's paralysing. You'll soon discover that not everyone is a fan of keeping it simple. Sadly, simplicity is often something people frown upon. One reason is that 'simple' gets confused with 'simplistic'. I promise you, keeping your leadership journey focused and simple will save you time, strife and stress.

Be warned. Keeping things simple will threaten people. They will think you're taking the easy route, you're lazy, looking for a shortcut, shallow or lacking understanding. Don't listen to them. 'Simple' simply means removing obstacles! If you're able to keep your leadership journey free from obstacles you'll run faster, jump longer and fly higher.

Leading with simplicity will produce transparency and accountability. Leading with complexity only creates hiding places. Don't leave a legacy of leading in the shadows.

As your leadership grows, perhaps the important question you could ask isn't 'what more can I do?' but 'what can I stop doing?' or even 'what can I change to achieve the same goal – by keeping it simple?' This is going to freak people out because they think leadership equals more work. They're wrong. Ignore them.

Just look around and you'll realise the simple things often have the most profound effect on our lives; a paper clip, a rubber band, Post-it notes, a pen and paper. One of my favourite quotes is the one about the Christmas tree: 'Like a Christmas tree, the more baubles and decorations that are hung upon it, the less you can see its original, simple shape.'

Every time you grow and find yourself stretched ask yourself this simple question: 'What has become so complex in my life that I have lost my original shape?'

Stay true to who you are as a leader and KISS as often as you can.

19.2.4 Character

leadership without good character is flawed

As a nineteen-year-old stepping into leadership for the first time, I knew nothing about the importance of character and how this influences my ability to lead others. After all, I was only nineteen and no one talked about this stuff. Nothing bothered me. It was all new to me; my main focus was purely on trying to figure out how to do stuff. *[Plus, I wanted to look good while I was doing it.]*

My behaviour at times can only be described as 'suspect'. My people skills were fairly 'nonexistent'. My attitude was pretty 'carefree'. Let's just say this, my leaders today would not get away with living like I lived and still be leaders.

Early days in leadership affords you some slack. I'm not sure how I got away with some stuff. *[Actually, as you are reading you will discover that I never did get away with it either.]* I know that twenty-five years on I am different. I am still not perfect, I still make mistakes but I am more aware now how my character has developed along the way. I am certain if it hadn't, then I would not be in a position of leadership today.

Character might not be the only thing I have had to pay attention to over the years, but it's definitely one of the most important. Good character builds trust, and trust is the foundation of great leadership. Added to competence and consistency, these are three of the ingredients which can help you become a really strong leader.

I have mentioned before how thankful I am for those who gave me a go. Especially for people like Kevin and Tina Hudson who spoke into my life in those early days, and many others since then. Those conversations have shaped me, challenged me, corrected me and grown me into who I am today. Making God central to the mix and the part He has played in my life too, reading the Word, hearing a message or responding to a call to the altar and I am more than I could have ever hoped to be based on my own efforts.

Good character does not appear overnight. It grows. It develops. It is nurtured. It is a choice. It is very much a discipline.

Here are some things that I have contributed to my learning when it comes to the development of my character . . .

1. Always be teachable
2. Learn from your mistakes
3. Read
4. Ask questions of the right people
5. Be willing to have the tough conversations
6. Admit when you are wrong
7. Practise
8. 'It's the way I am' is not a reason for poor character
9. Growing pains are uncomfortable
10. It's worth the investment – you will be a better person and leader

The character journey is possibly the most important one I have taken as a leader. People may have afforded me the occasional lapse in my levels of competence and ability. However, when your character comes into question, all you are doing is creating unnecessary cause for concern.

Let's unpack these throughout the following chapters.

to my 19-year-old self:

" You might say 'my character is just that – mine, so live with it.' To maintain your leadership over the long haul, the things in this list deserve attention. Everyone has character, just work at making sure people describe yours as good. **"**

questions:

Why do you think character is important in your leadership?

What, if anything, would you add to the list of things that can help build good character?

19.3 Teachable

leadership is about remaining teachable

___

At nineteen you are sure you don't need to learn anything. In your forties you are well aware that you still have a great deal to learn.

One thing I know for certain: leadership is a journey, not a destination. The moment you think you have made it or arrived is the moment you start to fail as a leader, and I never want to do that.

Tough though it can be, I am always looking for ways to

learn. I am not always happy about the process of learning but I have come to value it, as without new insights into who I am and how I lead, I have little or no chance of becoming a better leader. Once I say there is nothing you can teach me I am immediately placing a lid on my leadership effectiveness.

I have learned from my mistakes

Many, many mistakes, small or large, some I have been aware of, others made without even realising.

I have learned from not giving up on the journey

Failing doesn't make me a failure. Getting it wrong doesn't mean 'give up'. It is just another opportunity to learn how not to do something like that in the future.

I have learned from the wisdom and guidance of others

People close to me and from leaders across the globe, from within church settings and in business too.

I have learned from feedback

Always better to be invited and asked for, but still listen to the uninvited feedback too.

I have learned from my own leaders

From their experience, when they have said, 'No,' and when they have said, 'Well done.'

I have learned when made aware of my shortcomings

The right people with the permission to tell me to stop behaving like an idiot.

I have learned from reading books

Add to that attending conferences, listening to a podcast or taking a course.

I have learned by reading my Bible

I read with the attitude of observing what it says to me, looking at the person of Jesus Christ and with the desire to become more like Him. There is always room for improvement in this department.

Even in the last few days I have been learning about myself. I have listened to the words of others and had to ask the difficult questions of myself:

❙ Is there any truth in what they are saying?

❙ What can I learn to make me a better me?

No one ever said remaining teachable would be easy. I have discovered that to be dismissive of others, having a wrong attitude or just being plain ignorant, is not good enough and could see me disqualify myself as a leader.

Nobody likes to think they haven't quite got it right, but I believe good leaders grow through these times of honest reflection and I am determined to be that type of leader.

There is more to learn here when it comes to getting the right people around you. At times, everyone has an opinion. We can hear it but shouldn't always allow it to shape our future behaviour.

to my 19-year-old self:

" People will love to tell you how good or how bad you are at certain things, so learn to let them know you have heard them while becoming an expert at reflecting on what's been said without being held captive by those words. We can learn from anyone. Sometimes there may be some truth in it; other times, just ignore it. "

questions:

What have you learned by remaining teachable?

How willing are you to listen to what others say about you?

19.4 Mistakes

leaders make mistakes

You have to expect to make them. Any leader who says they have never made any mistakes is a liar.

Stepping into any leadership role means putting yourself out there, taking hold of responsibility and making decisions. Doing this can lead to mistakes. No one gets everything right every time. Plus, not everyone will agree with you either, for any number of different reasons. Maybe they consider you have acted too hastily or without due diligence. Sometimes it is because you have got it wrong (made that mistake); other times they feel this way because you are right and they just don't want to admit it.

Either way, a good leader recognises the potential for mistakes, works hard to eliminate them yet is also willing to learn and develop better self-awareness. We are all on this journey.

I'm sure others would be more than willing to share my misdemeanours but I'm going to get in first. Here is a list of some of mine. Though general in the writing, each one of these has a story attached. Each one represents people, individuals or a team, which could mean there is a hurt attached as well.

Disregarding the thoughts and feelings of other people. We are doing 'this'. This is me ploughing head-long into something without due care and attention to those it involves. What do they know anyway?

Not listening properly. Only being focused on what I think and not giving enough time to hear the views of my team. Too hands-on or too hands-off. This is bad leadership hidden under the guise of 'they need my help' or 'they just need to learn by having a go'.

Control, conveniently placed under the cover of systems and processes. Both are important but never more important than people. I have to work harder at this one too or my personality can take over.

Being in a hurry. Should have planned ahead more. Rushing is never a good excuse and can be the reason for most of the mistakes on this list.

Avoiding conversations, usually because they are the awkward and uncomfortable kind.

Lack of feedback. Both kinds – appreciation and correction when appropriate. I have missed the chance to give praise and appreciation when I should, as well as missing the chance to correct, too. This is just lazy leading.

Thinking only I know the answer. Simply code for arrogance.

Inappropriate lifestyle decisions. Too much being a leader who says, 'Do as I say,' not 'Do as I do.' Eventually those lifestyle issues will catch up on you.

Mistakes demonstrate our humanness. We are imperfect people, often not helped by those we lead expecting perfection. Mistakes are not pretty. When I think about some of those listed above, I cringe a little. In my early days of leadership I wasn't quick enough to recognise my mistakes, and I definitely didn't want to learn from them.

Nowadays, I do see the value in learning from the wrong, although that doesn't make admitting them any easier. In addition, I have learned to not only enjoy the benefits of grace shown towards me but to be as quick to show grace to others too.

to my 19-year-old self:

// Let's be real: you are going to make mistakes. This may be hard to imagine but you will be wrong. Discover the benefit of being willing to reflect on your mistakes. It builds credibility, develops your character, creates trust and will hopefully influence those you lead as they see your willingness to learn. **//**

questions:

What mistakes have you made in your leadership?

How have you learned from them?

leaders don't sweep mistakes under the carpet

When writing about learning from mistakes, maybe a follow-on would be useful. What do you really do when you make a mistake? As I write, I am given to think about a few obvious examples of mistakes from my own life, some of which I listed in the previous chapter.

Here are some observations about making mistakes I have

not necessarily learned the best way . . .

Seeing our own mistakes and openly admitting to them is a whole lot easier than the often unsolicited evaluation we receive from others. This is never comfortable but it happens a lot. It's amazing how much we enjoy informing others of their errors while not necessarily inviting the same type of feedback in respect of our own performance, and how we might improve ourselves.

There will always be someone else who thinks they are more suited to the job, able to lead things better, make wiser decisions, handle things more effectively, when in reality, it would simply be a different way of doing the same thing. Sometimes we have to trust ourselves, or if we are not the leader, we should put our energies into helping those that are. Alternatively, we could just acknowledge when we might be wrong and they might, in fact, be right.

To such individuals I would like to make three statements that normally as a leader we cannot actually make:

▌ Firstly, I acknowledge that my leadership mistakes may hurt you, but you need to know that when you get it wrong, it hurts me.

▌ Secondly, when leaders get it wrong, people love to tell them and others about it. When those we lead get it wrong and it hurts us, as good leaders we can't tell anyone.

▌ Finally, you think what I am choosing to do as the leader

is a mistake; however, it might be right and it just makes you uncomfortable because it is.

Here are nine suggestions of things to do when you know you've made a mistake . . .

Humble pie

Never tastes great but develop an appetite for eating it. It is vital you learn the art of humility, especially when you know you're not even wrong.

Smile and listen

For me this is usually done with my hands tightly clasped together behind my back, which stops me from waving them about when I want to respond.

Reflect

Is there any truth in what is being said to me? Is there something I need to learn from this and, if so, what action should I be taking in response?

Apologise

Many, many times, even if you don't feel you are in the wrong. Be the bigger person; say sorry and ask for forgiveness.

Forgive

Learn to let things go, don't hold a grudge. Not easy but very important. The danger is that, without choosing this response, we may become angry and bitter towards someone else who doesn't even realise they have upset us.

Be ready to change

Embrace the moment and become an even better leader.

Learn to understand that everyone is different

After all, everything we do is about people. We have to be able to see things from their perspective, to understand why they may be saying what they are saying. Be more focused on winning the person, rather than the argument.

Try to not say, 'Stuff It' and give up

Keep reminding yourself – don't quit.

Handle the consequences

Often you just have to take the hit. I have come out of mistakes with debt, a loss of trust, people leaving church, and friendships coming to an end. And other kinds of mess and the rebuilding which then has to be done.

You can't hide from the repercussions of a mistake, whatever it may look like. However, you can grow, learn, improve, regain trust and become a stronger, more credible leader. After all, God uses ALL things for the good of those who love Him and are called according to His purposes.

to my 19-year-old self:

" Excuse me for repeating myself, but you will make mistakes. Don't be so daft to think you never will. Most people understand this. The biggest thing you can learn is how best to respond to the mistakes, otherwise you will be unnecessarily disqualifying yourself from being a leader. **"**

questions:

What have been your best and worst experiences when it comes to mistakes you have made as a leader?

Would you add anything to the list?

leadership is about reading

This is not an original thought, many other leaders would say the same thing, but I have come to understand the truth behind the statement 'leaders are readers'.

At age nineteen my reading was for academic reasons. Alternatively, you were an old person who enjoyed good fiction. Twenty-five years on and I have disciplined myself to be an avid reader, getting through twenty-five to thirty books a year, on a whole manner of topics. The bulk will have a leadership focus, but then I read about people, marketing, social science, communication, Christianity, and building local church. I also enjoy a good autobiography, too, as it tells a particular person's journey and their learning along the way.

It all started in 1996. After sitting in a youth leaders' meeting discussing how to develop a bunch of potential leaders, it triggered a desire in me I didn't even realise I had. When we came back next time and the same conversation began, I was there with a ten-week course, which became 'Dreambuilders', the catalyst for my involvement in leadership development.

Four books changed the way I thought about what it meant to be a leader and how to handle those I was leading:

The 21 Irrefutable Laws of Leadership by John C. Maxwell

Developing the Leader Within You by John C. Maxwell

How to Win Friends and Influence People by Dale Carnegie

Courageous Leadership by Bill Hybels

Why read?
Knowledge
You don't know what you don't know. Reading helps widen our view and develop a greater understanding on much more than just the topics listed above. Plus, as a teacher/preacher they help when I am speaking too.

New ways of thinking about the same old things
What is the current thinking? This is important – otherwise I become out of touch, stuck in a past way of doing things,

which ultimately leads to irrelevance.

Inspiration
New ideas on some stuff I have never even thought about before. Gaining a wider view of the world I thought I knew.

Books, articles, blog posts, even podcasts can facilitate all of the above. Sometimes it's the whole thing which challenges me; other times it's been a chapter, an idea or maybe a single sentence. It really doesn't matter. What is important is always being on the lookout for ways to increase my understanding of what it means to be a leader and that's about more than just the practicalities. It's about continuing to learn about the type of person I need to become, to be a better leader.

For these reasons I will not stop reading.

When I look at my bookshelf here are some of my favourite reads, except for the four above would be . . .

Spiritual Leadership by J. Oswald Sanders

The Circle Maker by Mark Batterson

Great by Choice by Jim Collins

Making Ideas Happen by Scott Belsky

Mere Christianity by C.S. Lewis

Cracking Your Church's Culture Code by Samuel Chand

Outliers by Malcolm Gladwell

PUSH by Jurgen Matthesius

Axiom by Bill Hybels

Here are some thoughts that might help you increase your capacity to read more . . .

1. Pick an interesting book
Choose carefully. Make it something that you are pretty certain you will enjoy.

2. Get a book that is recommended

3. Choose something that is not so intimidating
For instance, you might prefer to begin with *The Next Generation Leader* by Andy Stanley as a good first leadership book to read, rather than *The Leadership Challenge* by Kouzes and Posner.

4. Set time aside to read
Doing this will help make it a discipline. Fifteen minutes a day is just over ninety hours a year which, based on the average read time for an average book, would mean you've read between twenty to twenty-five books in a year.

5. Use the chapters
They keep me on track, helping to set a target date for

completing the book. Larger books can often be easier to manage with this 'bitesize' approach.

6. Have it close at hand

Then you can read whenever. Some people have them in the car in case of traffic delays. Maybe even left by the toilet.

7. Have a list

And make it a BIG list.

8. Put it down

If you find it hard-going then leave it for a bit. Don't give it up altogether. This is where having a list helps. Move on to the next one then come back to it later.

9. Keep reading

It might be tough at first but keeping going always makes it easier next time.

10. Make notes/highlight

Don't lose the learning. Underline. Highlight. Journal. Whatever works best for you so you capture what gets your attention.

An extra thought: Learn to enjoy reading your Bible too

I know that can be an easy thing to say and not so easy to do but reading the Bible has to become a vital part of who you are as it will help you become all that God needs you to be. So how is your Bible reading going?

Here are five things which might just help you . . .

1. Get a version that you like – NIV, NKJV, ESV, The Message. There are many to choose from nowadays.

2. Have a Bible with you all the time. I use the Youversion app on my phone which means I can read wherever, whenever. You can download this app for free at youversion.com.

3. Bookmark, underline, journal the things that speak to you, make you think, challenge you or that you want to study further.

4. Try to keep to the plan. Consistency is the key. Don't worry if you miss a day; it's a plan not a legal requirement. Don't get discouraged.

5. Ask God to help you and to speak to you through what you are reading. Expect to hear from God.

to my 19-year-old self:

" Well done, you are reading a good book. Just keep picking something that will help you grow and keep going. No excuses. Learn to love reading because it is helping you to grow. It may not seem like much right now but over the next twenty-five years, wow, the difference could be unimaginable! **"**

questions:

What's your favourite leadership book and what did you learn from it?

What will you read next? Make a list.

stephen matthew

Speaker, coach, author and Principal of the Building Church Academy

Being nineteen was a big deal for me. I'd decided to study for my professional exams as a chartered surveyor by extension rather than attend university, which meant I could now make two other big decisions: to get married and to get involved deeply in a newly-formed church. Exciting times!

So in September 1975 the church was launched, and in October Kay and I got married. What I never anticipated at nineteen was that the confluence of those two decisions would shape the rest of my life.

I love my wife, our four adult children and soon-to-be eight grand-children more than I could ever describe. And I also love Jesus and His church with a passion; a passion that resulted in me entering full-time ministry for that church when I was just twenty-six.

However, the things we love will always compete; it is inevitable. So we must become very adept at balancing competing priorities and responsibilities. So my advice to my nineteen-year-old self would simply be: set your priorities now. Get God's perspective on all the things you legitimately love and make a strong decision to honour the priorities he teaches us to hold. Maybe then I would have been spared the pain of some of the mistakes I've made.

Youthful zeal, a strong responsibility ethic and a church environment that legitimised being a 'churchaholic' distorted my priorities over the years. So, I would look my nineteen-year-old self in the eye and make him repeat after me: 'God, Family, Church.'

Never let the order slip. Love God with all your heart, soul, mind and strength. Then love your wife and kids, always making the time to keep your Christ-centred family bond as strong as it can be. Then throw yourselves into helping Jesus build His church.

God will honour the hard choices you've sometimes to make between the competing things you love. Just never let the order slip: God, Family, Church.

19.6 Ask Questions

great leaders ask questions

Developing your leadership character is helped by asking the right questions.

I think the first question I asked was:'What am I doing?' Even now I still ask that question from time to time.

Here is another thing I have learned on my leadership journey that I would tell my nineteen-year-old self: *asking the right people the right questions at the right time has the ability to help you become the right kind of leader.*

It is something I am still not very good at so I have to work harder at it. When I was younger I think I was embarrassed to ask as I didn't want to look like I didn't know what I was doing. We have to get over this and understand that most people are actually thankful we have asked the question because they wanted the clarity too.

▌ Questions help you learn.

▌ Questions scratch beneath the surface.

▌ Questions are moments of genuine enquiry not just nosiness.

▌ Questions bring clarity.

▌ Questions grow you.

▌ Questions have answers we may not always want to hear but should listen to and learn from anyway.

You should always have a question. If you are listening to someone teach, get a question ready. You may not always get the chance to ask it but have one regardless.

To help you here are a few different sets of questions you could ask . . .

Leadership questions

What are the characteristics you look for in a leader?

What's the biggest thing you have learned about leadership?

Why do you think some leaders fail?

What do you do to keep growing as a leader?

What do you consider to be the most important decisions you make as a leader?

Growth questions

What have you been learning?

What is challenging you at the moment/where is the stretch?

Where do you still need to improve?

What is God saying to you?

Who do you have in your world who will pray with you?

Relationship with God questions

When was the last time I heard from God?

When was the last time I stood in faith for something?

When was the last time I put my reputation on the line for my faith?

When was the last time I sacrificed my agenda for God's?

How is my serving quotient? Is it based on what I consider convenient or based on a willingness to be inconvenienced by others?

Am I tithing?

Where am I struggling at the moment with sin?

If married, is my relationship with my spouse healthy? Have we prayed together? Have we spent time together? Are we talking?

Am I willing to deal with any unresolved issues that I am aware of?

Are my words encouraging, full of life and blessing or are they opinionated, negative and unnecessary?

Questions to ask about those around you

Do they believe in you?

Do they encourage you?

Do they inspire you?

Do they resource you?

Do they challenge you?

Do they ask the right questions?

Do they celebrate with you?

Do they have a great walk with God?

Do they demonstrate loyalty?

Do they trust you?

Do they share the same values and beliefs?

Heart questions

What would God find?

Would I be happy with what He found?

Why do I keep allowing things in my heart that just don't help me?

What can I do to change that?

Motive questions

Am I looking for approval?

Am I looking for personal recognition?

Am I looking for my own success?

Am I going after applause? Or ...

Will I just serve faithfully even if I never receive any public affirmation?

Will I give without any guarantee of return?

Will I put my trust in God and that my reward will come from Him?

to my 19-year-old self:

" Growing as a leader is all about learning. Through the things we do, from reading, from asking questions. So let me encourage you to be a leader who never thinks there is nothing to learn. You don't know it all so stop trying to be one. Nobody likes an arrogant leader. Ask questions – of yourself, of your team, and of other leaders, too. **"**

question:

If you could sit for a while with a leader who you want to learn from, who would it be and what questions would you ask?

19.7 Tough Conversations

leadership often involves hard conversations

I have already alluded to this topic when I wrote about confrontation. The whole journey as a leader is littered with mistakes, admitting or not to those mistakes, conversations, confrontation and a few difficult moments when questions have been asked.

From my own experiences I have learned how the tough conversations have been such an essential part of my leadership development journey...

1. Character develops when you are stretched

Learning how to handle tough conversations will definitely create moments of stretch. No one looks forward to this aspect of leadership development. How we respond shows what we are made of. Stretch is uncomfortable at the time but we can become stronger through the process.

2. The pressure of a tough conversation can be good for us

Not so much pressure that we are completely destroyed, but enough that we are broken. It can be through these moments of pressure where God can remake, reshape and mould us into the person He always intended us to become.

3. Tough conversations give greater opportunity for growth

We might not always like what we hear but if we respond correctly we will be the better for it. The choice is ours whether we become bitter or better from the experience. Whether we grow as a leader or grind to halt as a leader. Tough conversations could be viewed as pivotal moments – do you work through it or do you quit?

4. Take the hit

At age nineteen a lot of the conversations about my leadership were tough. I don't think I really listened. As a nineteen-year-old I felt invincible. However, I do remember sitting in the kitchen of my leaders' house and them asking the simple question, *'Is this true?'* I took the hit and it saved me. I wouldn't be a leader in the way I am today if I had only allowed it to knock me down and not got back up again.

5. Always be honest

Cover up, blagging it, telling a lie, hoping a half-truth is enough, or denial – none of them work. Honesty remains the best policy. Get whatever is being talked about into the open, dealt with, and then you can begin to move on.

Good leaders will receive the conversation with the intention of seeing the issue resolved and not return to it again, unless we take them there again through our own repeated behaviour.

Now I am on the other side of the equation and find myself as a leader having these tough conversations with future leaders and I endeavour to make sure I keep the following in mind . . .

▌ To not be too harsh or judgemental.

▌ To remember I was a young leader once.

▌ Everyone misses the mark at times.

▌ To look for where the change can be made and encourage them towards it.

▌ To make sure they know I still believe in them. Failing does not have to be fatal.

❚ To win the person not just the confrontation.

It's about grace and truth. Too much truth and we hurt people. Too much grace and we don't learn about the consequences of our actions. It's about truth with a way through.

to my 19-year-old self:

" You idiot. That you even put them in the situation where the conversation was needed. Behave yourself. But, in the knowledge that you will make some daft choices, get ready for the 'chat'. When it happens, listen, learn, nod your head, don't try and cover it up. In doing so, you help them to be able to help you move on in your leadership journey. **"**

questions:

What's your experience of tough conversations?

How do you handle them now?

Are you doing something right now which could lead to one of these tough conversations?

19.8 Heart

be a leader who knows how to keep their heart right

The other evening with a bunch of young leaders I was asked a great question – what has been your biggest leadership challenge and how did you overcome it?

For a moment I struggled. Not that I have never had a challenge in my leadership, but when you reflect on a question like this it can be difficult to articulate your answer. All along my leadership journey there have been times of challenge, you just don't always realise it. If you're anything like me, you've just got on with it and, with God's help, overcome them.

My answer (prompted by my wife) was '2008'.

The leadership challenge in 2008 was this – I could have left church. I thought I was exactly where God wanted me to be. Then, without notice, things changed. A combination of events knocked me, which created a challenge I am convinced that all of us will go through at some point. What will I do in response to what has been done to me, to what has offended me?

All I can say is that there will be moments like this for you. Guaranteed. Someone is going to say something, do something, respond in a way that upsets you, or something you have been doing will be taken from you. An 'unexpected event' that will ask questions of your motives, your values and, quite likely, your faith. And this is without even thinking of the mistakes we make ourselves. Somehow I chose to respond in the right way.

Well, I hear you cry, that's easy for you, you're a pastor. Not sure why people think that way. I'm just a normal person who gets upset about the same kind of stuff that everyone else gets upset by.

This is not about me bragging. Looking back, the reason I

survived that challenge, and therefore my family survived, was because my heart was not going to be moved. At some point previously I had determined that, come what may, my heart will not be moved.

My heart is for God. My heart is for my family. My heart is for His church. My heart is for Xcel Church. It is my home and I have no intention of leaving home. I don't ever want me or my family to be homeless.

On reflection, 2008 wasn't really that much of challenge because I had already passed tests on other occasions. I just hadn't realised it. Yet when I look back on my life I can see the times when my heart was tested.

1998: Some difficult work stuff as a Financial Adviser.

1999: Would I move to London for a job?

2001: A huge step of faith.

2003: Looking for some extra income which led to a 'miracle' job.

Then 2008. And since then, some even bigger challenges that have tested my heart. My only advice, especially to those who lead – choose today where your heart should be and then stay there. I have learned that there is nothing SO big where God is not BIGGER, that He cannot help me overcome.

Psalm 15 puts it like this . . .

> 'Lord, who may dwell in your sanctuary? Who may live on your holy hill? He whose walk is blameless and who does what is righteous, who speaks the truth from his heart and has no slander on his tongue, who does his neighbour no wrong and casts no slur on his fellow-man, who despises a vile man but honours those who fear the Lord, who keeps his oath even when it hurts, who lends his money without usury and does not accept a bribe against the innocent. He who does these things will never be shaken.'

▌ Staying humble stops me from being offended.

▌ Staying humble stops me from making emotion-led decisions.

▌ Staying humble keeps my own motives in check.

▌ Staying humble reminds me that God is always on the throne of my life.

In *The Leadership Challenge*, Posner and Kouzes evidenced that the number-one thing people look for in a leader is honesty, which is why humility, remaining humble, is so important. Admitting our mistakes, knowing our own limits, seeking guidance, and appreciating the input and success others bring, all help us stay humble and create that all important sense of trust.

▌ Humility is not a weakness although when we start out in leadership we often see it that way.

▌ Humility is important when it comes to handling mistakes well but probably even more important when it comes to handling success. Remember, no one likes bad losers or bad winners.

▌ Humility builds your credibility. We just don't like that it takes so long. You can't fake it. False humility just doesn't stand the test of time. If you are unwilling to be humble then you may fall because of pride.

▌ Humility involves being honest, which is another reason why we don't always enjoy it.

▌ Humility is saying, 'I don't know everything.'

▌ Humility thinks of others, the team, and those I lead. It doesn't think of me, my 'self'. People buy-in to someone who shows themselves to be humble. And that's leadership.

You can be a humble leader and still lead with strength. You can be a humble leader and still enjoy success. Genuine humility is an attractive quality in any leader, you just have to be determined to stick at it. It can take a very long time before people talk about you that way.

to my 19-year-old self:

" This is about becoming a great leader, not just a good one. You will experience roaring success and abject failure. These will be because of you and because of others. Remember, it is not about you. Don't become over-confident in your abilities, it could well be your downfall. Stay humble. Recognise that, without God and without others, any success you have means very little. **"**

questions:

How has a lack of humility tripped you up in your leadership?

How could humility help you in the future?

19.8.1 An Honest Moment

one of those pivotal leadership moments

I recently visited the couple who I lived with in Sheffield when I was at university. I cannot express how much of a blessing Hil and Ed Grundy have been to me and my family over the years. They are just a beautiful couple who are an example of how to love God, love family and love others.

It's a long story how me living with them came about but here goes ...

I didn't get into the halls of residence because of a postal strike, ended up living with a Methodist minister after my dad, also a Methodist minister, had made some calls. When I ended up dating his daughter, this lovely couple offered me a room.

Suffice to say, God moves in mysterious ways. It is through this convoluted mix of events I got involved in leadership with the young people at the church in Sheffield in the first place; we took them to the church in Newton Aycliffe, where I met a beautiful young lady who would eventually become my wife. The rest, as they say, is history.

Visiting them reminded me of one very awkward but extremely rewarding day. I was twenty-one and had been confronted by my leaders about some wrong lifestyle decisions which I couldn't actually deny. I had lied, covered up, behaved badly and now it had all caught up with me when allegations were made. Uncomfortable is an under-statement. It's hard to express the sick feeling in the pit of your stomach at a moment like this.

I have debated with myself as to whether I should include this part of my story or not. Looking back, though, this was a pivotal moment for me; one which, depending on how I responded, would influence the rest of my life, not just my leadership right then and there but into the future too.

There are lots of options when you get confronted, I have talked about this already. I'm pretty certain that curl up and die was somewhere on the list. Yet I did not. Instead, my response was to do something that I could only have done by the power of the Holy Spirit. Even now, I can't quite believe I actually did what I did.

It was the hardest thing I have ever done.

It was the best thing I have ever done.

What did I do? I went round to all those I loved and who loved me and said sorry, repented and asked them for forgiveness. Deliberate sit-down conversations with my parents, with Hil and Ed, with Kevin and Tina, with my best friends and anyone else who I could think I needed to be completely honest with.

It was a journey of repentance and forgiveness which was excruciatingly difficult but beautifully liberating at the same time. To my nineteen-year-old self I have to remind you, this situation only came about through my own arrogance and pride, and they can happen to just about anyone, if you are not careful.

Be ready to repent. Be ready to ask for forgiveness. These two might be the greatest defence of your leadership and potential for God than any other thought in this book.

▌ Repentance breaks the hold of whatever it is that has a hold of you.

▌ Repentance disarms those things which can sabotage your God-given potential.

▌ Repentance brings the truth out into the open where it can then be dealt with.

▌ Repentance gives God permission to get involved and to turn things around.

▌ Repentance leads to forgiveness which leads to an outpouring of grace which sets you up for the future.

▌ Repentance reminds you how much God loves you and how much those closest to you love you as well.

There were tears during those conversations but there was freedom too. There was some time out for me from leading but there was a future. One which has kept me on the journey with God, getting better not bitter, living out the plans and purposes He has for my life and enjoying the adventure of building people and building local church.

to my 19-year-old self:

// You may not see this coming but when it does be ready and willing to repent. It will be difficult and awkward, however, it will save you. To become a leader still making a difference twenty-five years from now, how you navigate such a moment will be a determining factor. **//**

questions:

What might be going on in your life that you need to repent of?

Take some time with God and allow the Holy Spirit to nudge you and then deal with it; bring it out into the open and walk into your future completely free.

practise your leadership

Sounds like one of those daft things to say but to become a better leader and to develop the right characteristics, you need to practise.

When I was younger I played a number of sports to quite a good level. I played badminton for the county. I competed in the Sussex Open Snooker Tournament. I played tennis for the local club.

I had some ability but I never broke through and the reason for this is simple: I didn't like the practice.

▌ Practice was boring and repetitive.

▌ Practice was not glamorous.

▌ Practice wasn't competitive.

▌ Practice was time-consuming.

▌ Practice was about coaching, being corrected, being told about every little thing that wasn't quite right.

However, on the flip-side . . .

▌ Practice was essential.

▌ Practice was about improving.

▌ Practice was about messing up when it didn't matter.

▌ Practice was about increasing my chances for success in the future.

▌ Practice was about learning new techniques and keeping up to date.

I am thankful for the opportunities presented to me as a nineteen-year-old to learn what leadership was about. To be encouraged to have a go. For all intents, to be allowed to practise. What I have learned on the journey, the things I am sharing with you on these pages, have definitely played a major role in shaping me into the leader I am today.

The practice has taken many forms and many roles . . .

I have set out and put away more chairs than I can even count. For a season I was the caretaker at church. Why? Not because it's my 'gifting'; purely because it needed to be done and I could do it.

I have arrived first and stayed last at so many events.

I have picked up litter.

I have dealt with the press, with complaints from neighbours. I have even had to stop someone blocking the car park while our Christmas Eve service was happening.

I have cleared and landscaped gardens, painted fences and cleaned homes, including dog poo from someone's backyard.

I have driven the van, the bus, taken rubbish to the council tip.

I have dealt with midnight call outs, fires in the building and even been head-butted while doing street work.

I have led and taught in Sunday school and kids' church.

I have been involved as a youth leader.

I have the opportunity to lead congregations and all

that is a part of pastorally caring for people.

I don't share all these to show off; I share them to illustrate how all of them are practice moments. Each of them has made me a better leader as each of them has provided opportunities to learn something new: new things about me, about people and about what it takes to build local church.

To help you practise your leadership here are some thoughts about how to practise and how it can help you become a better leader . . .

▌ Practice is a part of the process needed to help you perfect your leadership art.

▌ Practice provides opportunities for you to rehearse the leadership role to get it right.

▌ Practice is a chance to apply those new techniques as you learn them.

▌ Practice creates time to consider all the options.

▌ Practice can help you take on those common, tried-and-tested leadership skills you are becoming aware of.

▌ Practice is about implementing others' ideas which may improve your performance.

▌ Practice will bring times of pause, to check your motives and to ask questions like why are you wanting to improve?

❚ Practice is mostly about exercising your leadership muscles and stretching yourself when appropriate.

to my 19-year-old self:

// This is important to learn. Practice, practice, practice. Just keep doing what you can. Even the world's greatest athletes still practise so why would you think this principle doesn't relate to all walks of life? **//**

questions:

What do you think to my idea of practising your leadership?

How would you go about doing this?

leadership excuses just don't work

It wasn't an interrogation although at the time it may have felt like it. There was no light shining in my face. There was no lie detector test. It was just me on one side of the table and my leaders on the other. I felt a little flushed, awkward, uncomfortable; the meeting was generating a healthy glow as my brow perspired.

A question came, 'So, how did it go?'

Answered, at a ridiculously fast pace, 'Great. It was great.

Really good. Fantastic. All good.'

Reply, with a knowing lilt, 'Really?'

Answered more thoughtfully, with a good shrug of the shoulders, 'Well, it wasn't my fault, I can explain, it shouldn't have happened that way. The team got it wrong. In actual fact, so-and-so messed up.'

❚ It's not my job

❚ That was someone else

❚ Yes, but I can explain

❚ Didn't know I had to

❚ The team let me down

❚ It wasn't that bad really

❚ I don't have enough time

❚ It wasn't the right time

❚ The effort wasn't worth it

❚ We are not ready

❚ It wasn't affordable

With an eagerness to please and to succeed, excuses can

be the quickest and simplest reply for when something hasn't quite gone the way it should have done.

These are what Craig Hickman, Roger Connors and Tom Smith in their book *The Oz Principle* would describe as a 'below the line' attitude. Playing the blame game.

Excuses for why things went wrong or for why we didn't do something come in many shapes and sizes. I've probably used all of those listed above and more. Let's be honest, we have all used them and there is no shortage of creativity when it comes to excuses. We like to save face, to give reasons for non-action that sound reasonably plausible. Either way, when we get called to account, it can be an uncomfortable conversation.

Excuses demonstrate a lack of ownership, a lack of determination on our part to do things right but they can also create a lack of progress too. Passing the blame is an easier option than taking responsibility. However, in doing so we lose credibility and eventually we will lose the right to lead others. Leaders can give away just about anything, except ultimate responsibility.

So, what have I learned on the journey when it comes to leadership and excuses? They don't help me develop as a leader, except to learn that they don't help me. After all, leadership is about getting things done and excuses are just reasons for why I haven't got done what I said I would get done.

I am endeavouring to always stay above the line, to stick to the principles laid out in *The Oz Principle* which will help break these patterns of behaviour. To be willing to be held accountable and actually ask for accountability. I talk about this in a later chapter.

Hickman, Connors and Smith suggest four steps anyone can take as an alternative approach to the normal excuses . . .

See It
Recognise that you fall below the line and how you fall below the line.

Own It
Take ownership of these and be ready to act.

Solve It
Yes, find solutions but also the willingness to battle through with that solution.

Do It
Make the solution a reality and be kept accountable for the outcomes you desire.

to my 19-year-old self:

" Avoid being known as the leader who always has an excuse. Ask to be held accountable. An inattention to results and the behaviours that influence them although easier will not help you to grow as a leader. **"**

questions:

What's your favourite excuse?

How can you make sure you don't allow excuses to stop you?

leaders need to grow

If I was having a conversation today about leadership with my nineteen-year-old self I would probably see someone with a bit of bravado, with some 'assumed' coolness *[because I wasn't that cool, I just thought I was]*, a person with a very laid-back approach to life, and a possible disregard to having to talk to someone older who might actually know something that could help them as they start out in leadership.

you will need to grow

Five simple words. That is what I would say to myself.

It's what this whole book is about. I'm pretty certain I got told this. Actually, I'm fairly certain my leaders may well have just told me to 'grow up' but the sentiment would have been the same. **Growth as a leader is essential.**

Sometimes I have fought the need to grow. Other times I have embraced it. I have willingly and unwillingly listened to others who definitely knew better. John C. Maxwell writes about the *Law of the Lid* and how our leadership ability is the 'lid' that determines our effectiveness. With this in mind, I have banged my head on my own leadership lid more times than I can remember.

Each time this has happened I have had to decide – do I grow as a leader, increase my capacity or do I just stay where I am and lose my leadership role eventually to the ones who have decided to keep on growing?

Here's what I am still learning about how to grow as a leader . . .

Growth is best when it's gradual

Don't try and get there in a day. Becoming a better leader takes time. I have been in some form of leadership for over twenty-five years and I am still developing, learning, changing and growing. You never reach perfection as a leader. Just keep on looking for that improvement.

I'm not big into exercise. I need to get better. Playing squash recently, for the first time in about ten years, taught me

leaders need to grow

that not warming up or stretching out your muscles beforehand can cause problems – I couldn't move properly for a few days after playing! Stretching is important to help become stronger physically. The same is true in leadership. I have learned that to keep growing I have had to keep looking for opportunities where I will be challenged and stretched.

Growth must happen

Without growth we are stagnating. We are saying, 'I don't need to learn anymore, I have arrived.' We never arrive.

At nineteen I may not have realised there was a need to grow. Now I recognise I need to be growing all the time.

If you don't want to be a leader anymore, just stop growing yourself and see what happens.

Growth needs to be internal

Talent is great, but character is greater. People may follow talent for a while but, over the longer term, they follow the person. What makes the person who they are is what others follow. Leadership is about much more than the successful completion of a task.

It's a fight sometimes but we all know where we need to grow. Be honest with yourself. Acknowledge your strengths. Make them stronger and become an expert in them. Accept your weaknesses too. Don't just ignore them. Develop the ones that link to your leadership character, your integrity and your trustworthiness, rather than the talent aspect, although you may need to do that too.

Growth, or lack of it, will become evident eventually

Others may recognise our growth or lack of it before we do. It only really becomes visible when we get tested in the area we needed to have grown in. The 'next time' will tell us the truth about how we are doing.

Like it or not, I have found that having people in my world who I am 'happy' to hear the truth from helps me. I'm not always 'happy' with what they might say but I am even less happy with being found out in my leadership by others who just love to tell me about my failings. *'Faithful are the wounds of a friend'* (Proverbs 27:6 KJV).

All this raises the question of how do I grow as a leader? Well, reading this book should be a good place to start. Take time to reflect with the questions, read some good leadership books, ask more questions, keep going, and get some good leaders around you who can create opportunities for stretch and growth.

to my 19-year-old self:

" Grow up! You're nineteen for goodness' sake. You don't know enough to think there is nothing to learn. Everything is a test, a learning opportunity. Nothing is wasted so never despise all you are doing yourself or how others could invest in you. Grow, grow, and grow some more. **"**

questions:

What would you add to the list about why growing as a leader is important?

Where would you say growth is needed in your own leadership?

leaders need accountability

One of the key things I have learned in twenty-five-plus years of leadership is this: **accountability is not just a good idea, it's an absolute must.**

I know I'm in danger of repeating myself but when you're young you really don't see the need for accountability. It's such a boring sounding word. 'I don't need 'wisdom' from someone older.' 'I don't want to be asked, 'How are you doing?'' 'No one can tell me anything and certainly not teach me anything'. 'I will just learn from my own mistakes and so be it'. These are all phrases I have actually heard people use. We can be right in our own mind if we want but that doesn't make us a good leader. Accountability is about taking responsibility for our actions. It helps us to not be arrogant, which is never an attractive quality.

Leaders who don't look for and welcome some form of accountability are setting themselves up to fail. Or are fooling themselves and convincing themselves that the excuses they are using are actually true.

I am totally convinced I would not have survived in leadership if it hadn't been for the voice of reason, the voice of responsibility and the voice of right-thinking, coming primarily from my own leaders, from people I looked up to and respected, and from people who wanted me to improve and who believed in me.

The voice of reason asks me the right questions

This person (or group of people) has permission to ask questions which go further than what are you doing or how did it go?

Instead they probe deeper with 'why' are you doing this? If you keep behaving like this where will it lead? How can you do things differently to get a better result?

This person asks the big 'what if' type questions. They challenge my motives. And if they are the right kind of people they will ask me questions about my faith in God too.

The voice of responsibility keeps me safe within the right kind of boundaries

I learnt that to not listen to others who have gone before me is a display of monumental ignorance. Ignorant people think they don't need any boundaries, which only leads to a whole bunch of issues which could have been avoided – lack of clarity, lack of engagement and focus, confusion, demotivation of the team, lack of identity, ill-conceived choices – all of which lead to a breakdown in trust and a loss of respect for you as the leader.

I've caused many of these over the last twenty-five years just because I chose not to be attentive to what my leaders were saying and we haven't even begun to mention any personal misbehaviours or crossing of inappropriate boundaries.

This person wants me to succeed. The boundaries they may set or suggest are not there to harm me but to cause me to flourish. Not just focused on the 'what's wrong' but even more they are focused on what is right and encouraging me to 'go for it'.

The voice of right-thinking helps me grow in wisdom

It's not about listening to every voice but considering what the right people have to say. Both their successes and their mistakes are full of the best wisdom. I know this works for me now as a leader when I'm thinking of what to pass on to others.

I am absolutely certain that these voices have influenced and benefited me in at least three areas of my leadership . . .

▐ in my behaviour – the type of leader I have become

▐ in my growth – the fact I am still in leadership all these years later

▐ in my aptitude – the skills I have as a leader

These people bring experience into my life and want me to learn from it. The key for me is to always have both a desire and willingness to listen to what they are saying.

to my 19-year-old self:

" Remember, you've not arrived, you've just been given a go by someone who believes in you. Make the most of them and other leaders in your world, people who can speak into your life. They are those who will hold you accountable, not only in terms of competence but more essential, with regard to your character, with the 'who' and not just the 'what'. "

questions:

How could being accountable to another leader have a positive influence on your leadership?

Who would this person be for you?

19.13 Layers Not Levels

leadership is about layers not levels

I think in my early days as a leader I thought leadership was about being important. It was about rising to the next level. A new fancy title. A more important title. A title on a badge is always better, or a lanyard, that's extremely official. If we are honest, we've all thought like this at some point.

Joking apart, though, this was a serious discovery for me on my leadership journey. The title tricked me into thinking that was who I really was. That getting to the 'next level' was what it was all about. It massaged my ego to be the leader of the youth group, especially when it was called JCs. It meant I had access, I could make decisions about what we would do. Don't you mess with what's going on here, I'm in charge.

Don't get me wrong, I was never a bossy leader. I'm not really a flashy person but, looking back on some pictures of me as a leader then, I definitely thought I was IT. Trying to be cool when I so wasn't.

There was a danger the title was inflating my own sense of importance, making me think more highly of myself than I probably should have done.

Honesty time . . .

We love a good title.

We love to know we have a position.

We love that our talent is getting us noticed.

Yet none of these things really made me the leader. They are all important but none of these things made ME important. They might help me to rise into a leadership position but ultimately may not be enough to keep me in the leadership position when I get kicked, pushed, prodded, challenged, confronted, hurt, picked on, accused and feel unloved as the leader.

The level we have attained can only protect us for a while. It's the layers on our leadership which truly keep us safe, and will help us continue on our journey of leadership.

▌ Layers are not flashy.

▌ Layers are not cool.

▌ Layers are often seen as unnecessary.

▌ Layers are boring.

I remember climbing Helvellyn, a mountain in the Lake District, and being told that the best thing to wear was lots of layers, and I'm glad I did. I carried my waterproof trousers and jacket in my backpack. I was prepared for all eventualities. The sun beat down on us when we began the walk but at the top, the wind was blowing, it was much cooler and when the rain came I was thankful for those extra layers hidden away in my bag.

Leadership layers are just the same. Not always needed but there. Often not seen, unless called upon. Layers increase our influence as a leader, more than our title ever will. We will find ourselves being invited to the conversation not just because of what we do but for who we have become.

We have journeyed through the levels of leadership without even realising. From being followed because of position in the first instance, to being followed just because of who we are, and what our life is actually producing.

I think about leaders I look up to and many of them have never led me because of a title. It is who they are, how they live life, how they lead and the centrality of their faith in God which makes me listen to them and want to follow their example.

I am sure that different leaders would name different layers but here are seven for starters . . .

❚ The layer of discretion

❚ The layer of integrity

❚ The layer of attitude

❚ The layer of trustworthiness

❚ The layer of credibility

❚ The layer of reliability

❚ The layer of ownership

These are the areas that often are neglected in the pursuit of the next level or title but are the areas I believe any leader should be paying most attention to.

to my 19-year-old self:

" People talk about moving to the next level. My suggestion is get past this idea. Put your energies into concentrating on the layers of leadership. Then the progression and promotion you desire are more likely to take care of themselves. **"**

questions:

Hope you agree. Which layers do you need to work on?

What extra layers would you add to your leadership?

what would you tell your 19-year-old self about leadership?

scott wilson

Founder of ICLM, President of Eurolead.net

If I could go back to age nineteen, which is a good forty years back, what would I say to my nineteen-year-old self? It's a great question but, frankly, I didn't need too much time to think about it as I have asked this question of myself many times.

I would ask, and I would suggest all new Christians are taught the answer to this, 'How do I do this for seventy years?' I've seen too many Christians, leaders and good people give up on their faith but especially commitment to leadership in short spaces of time for the strangest of reasons.

I would call this idea Leadership Longevity which is supported by the process of Sustainability. Longevity is about carrying yourself in a way that can last the distance. It deals with the way you handle work, ministry, family and difficult times in life. It starts with biblical values and good decision making.

Sustainability is to determine if the pace and choices of life I make are truly able to be maintained. Sustainability asks of all process and decision, can I do this for the rest of my life, or at least long term? It would ask, what are the results of this process and decision? It would ask who else can sustain this with me?

An example of this is Christian marriage. When a couple meet and pursue the decision to create a life together, is it all emotionally based or can it really be sustained for the rest of their lives?

It's possible that if people thought this way the church would be bigger, better and filled with happy, content people.

leaders know when to speak

Here's my simple thought on discretion – **you need it.**

As a leadership layer it will protect you. If you want to fail in leadership then be a leader who demonstrates a distinct lack of discretion. Not many people want to follow someone like that.

The dictionary tells us *discretion* is the quality of behaving or speaking in such a way as to avoid causing offence or revealing confidential information.

In the book of Proverbs we are told that *'discretion will*

preserve you'. We understand this statement and how important it is yet I am amazed how many times I have watched people learn about it the hard way. In other words, through not using it.

▌ We open our mouths too soon.

▌ We pass on information which was not ours to pass on.

▌ We give opinions even if others don't want to hear them.

▌ We speak over people just to be heard.

▌ We share half-truths.

▌ We exaggerate, and stretch the truth.

▌ We lack the ability to know what to do with what we know.

▌ We share a light-hearted comment which in all honesty is just unnecessary.

Many years ago I attended a youth leaders' conference. I can only remember one thing from it that has stood me in good stead for the past twenty-five-plus years. It's a simple phrase, one which has become an essential filter for me in leadership and how to handle what I hear . . .

who needs to know?

In over twenty-five years of leadership I have discovered

that on most occasions the answer to this question is this
... **not as many as I think**. Actually, it's most often no
one. We struggle with knowing something. We feel the
need to pass it on but once it's out there it's practically
impossible to get it back.

We have the right to remain silent, but seemingly lack
the ability to do so.

I am no expert and I know that I may still get this wrong
on occasion but a layer of discretion has kept me on the
leadership pathway ...

▌ I have learned to temper my opinion. To think it through.

▌ I have learned to not pass on what I know just because I
know.

▌ I have developed the ability to be discreet. To keep
knowledge confidential.

▌ I have noticed over the years how people don't come to
me for the up-to-date gossip.

▌ I am trying to no longer give my opinion only because I
have one.

▌ I am listening first and learning to respond more
carefully.

In some instances I have been too quiet and had to be
reminded that I wasn't invited to a meeting to only make

up the numbers. I am supposed to speak. I guess my adage has often been 'less is more'. Although I have become braver over the years.

It's hard to instruct you on how to become a person of discretion but if you can master it, if you can learn to keep your mouth closed when in the past it opened too freely, then your influence as a leader has the potential to increase greatly.

to my 19-year-old self:

" Discretion will keep you. This may be difficult to understand right now but here goes: speak less, listen more. Just because you can say something doesn't mean you should. Think it through. Better to wait to be asked than to launch in. Stop talking over everyone like your opinion is the only one that truly matters. Remember, people don't like a know-it-all. **"**

questions:

What are the challenges to living with discretion?

But what are the benefits to being a leader with great discretion?

19.15 Integrity

leaders without integrity are incomplete

Continuing this idea of how leadership is not about levels but more about layers. Multiples of different layers. The challenge with layers is they take time. A level can possibly be won quickly, through a promotion or just because someone else quits. It doesn't always mean you have what it takes for people to want to follow you.

Layers are not so much about what you do but more about why you do it. They are defining who you are. They are your character and people follow your character, you as a person, the who and the why, more than they do the what.

At nineteen, integrity isn't one of those topics you think about. I know I didn't. If I had, I would have been more conscious of how I lived a very hypocritical lifestyle. I was doing leadership as a role but it was just something I did, it wasn't who I was. At least not yet. At nineteen, when I first stepped into leadership, I didn't really understand how everything is connected. How even though I can be successful at the doing, if another aspect of who I am is in competition with that, then ultimately I am failing.

Just think about politicians, or some sportsmen and women. Too often their performance is outstanding but they fail miserably in being people you would choose to follow. They possess great talent but they are severely lacking in good character. They lack integrity.

I am not perfect. Wasn't at nineteen and, even though more than twenty-five years have now passed, I'm still not. In the beginning I didn't consider my integrity but I do now. It's taken over twenty-five years to earn it, to grow it as a layer. My awareness of how some foolish moments will give my integrity a hefty dent or see me lose it completely has improved. The specific accountability of good leaders in my life, which I have referenced in other chapters, has been a contributing factor rather than just my own personal opinion or that of a couple of mates.

▌ Integrity takes time.

▌ Integrity has a cost.

▌ Integrity covers everything.

▌ Integrity is a choice.

▌ Integrity is a personal discipline.

Like most of these layers, I can't make you a person of integrity; I can only sell you the benefits.

▌ No skeletons in the cupboard.

▌ No awkward conversations.

▌ No moments of indecision.

▌ No double-mindedness.

▌ No more living two different lives.

Integrity helps make sure our yes is yes and our no is no. Boundary lines for our life and how we will live are set when we have integrity. We know who we are and other choices have to line up with them. It doesn't mean we don't care about others but it does mean that sometimes what we care about has to come first.

Integrity comes from our why and it influences our what and our how. The why of my life is built on my Christian faith and the lifestyle that Jesus would ask me to live. I want my life to be whole and complete, in line with the word of God, thereby helping me maintain my integrity.

I didn't realise it at the time but when I went around asking parents, leaders and friends to forgive me, what I was really doing was protecting my integrity, or at least beginning the rebuilding process *[see 19.8.1]*.

If you desire to be a leader who others want to follow, then work on your integrity. Who you are when no-one else sees. In word, in deed, in every facet of your life.

If you want help in unpacking this idea further then I would recommend a book by Dr Henry Cloud called *Integrity*. Read it with a willingness to be honest about yourself, to make the hard calls and make changes if necessary. Identify those areas where you lack integrity and start unpacking a new layer of leadership. It will make so much difference, you will wonder why you never did this before.

As I often say to others when I'm teaching them about leadership, character and integrity, *'Everything is a test'*. I'm not sure they always believe me but how you deal with or respond at those critical moments will either increase your leadership capacity or put a limit on it. Maybe in a few years you can tell me if I'm right.

to my 19-year-old self:

" You can't ignore integrity. You can't just say, 'Well this is me, so people will have to get over it.' Integrity matters. Integrity cares. How you act, especially as a Christian leader, doesn't only reflect on you, but also on what you lead, where you lead and ultimately on God. So please be more careful. **"**

questions:

How could you improve your own integrity?

Why not find someone who is a leader you respect and ask them to help you become a leader with greater integrity.

19.16 Attitude

your attitude will determine your influence

In all of my leadership experiences, attitude has been one of the steepest learning curves.

At nineteen I had a fairly carefree attitude. You've probably picked that up already. I was only really a leader by title and position rather than a leader in lifestyle. That's the journey I have travelled and will continue to travel until I go to heaven.

Attitude is caught not taught. It's not easy to teach others what the right attitude is for life's multitude of circumstances. What works for one doesn't always work for another.

Here are five things you could choose to do when it comes to improving your own attitude . . .

1. Learn by observing others

Find some leaders you admire or consider have a right attitude. Maybe you share some of the same values.

When I reflect on my leadership journey, I am thankful for different individuals and leaders who have displayed the right kind of attitude at the right time. I have watched how they have handled people, coped with awkward moments, as well as learning about money from them or even how to raise great kids and a myriad of other necessary life skills

2. Learn by getting it wrong

Not deliberately, that's just daft. Looking back on my leadership I can clearly see times when getting it wrong could have led me to become negative, overly cynical, even angry, towards others and towards myself too. None of these attitudes are healthy. The end results could have seen me implode or quit.

Instead, realise we all make mistakes and that it's the right kind of attitude which can help us through those times. With the help of others and, more importantly, with the help of God, I have been able to maintain a positive attitude, one which helped me learn from what went wrong. I have become a leader who can make adjustments along the way and actually become better from the experience.

3. Learn by surrounding yourself with the right kind of like-minded people

Friends will encourage you to keep going when you may consider giving up. Don't forget to return the favour when they need a friend. You only need one or two of the right kind of friends but they might make all the difference in your ability to survive as a leader.

We also need other leaders in our world who will give us a friendly kick too. Sometimes we won't even realise they are doing this. Words of encouragement, support, prayer and the odd challenge along the way are great ways to help build the right attitude.

4. Learn by always thinking of others first

Leadership is about serving. Someone once said that you never graduate from serving. It does mean that you are not always right. I have learned that the attitude of 'just do it because I'm the leader' rarely wins people's hearts. First, serve them, willingly.

Those who gave me my first opportunity have told me how this was one of the key reasons they chose me. I didn't push myself forward but rather encouraged others to have a go. They saw in me a servant heart, a person with an attitude of care and love towards others.

The challenge is working hard to protect this kind of attitude as we grow older.

5. Learn that you'll never stop learning

It's been said many times by many people, leadership is a journey not a destination. Once you think you've got this attitude stuff sorted and attained to some kind of untouchability, that could be the moment you start heading for a fall.

If my attitude determines my leadership influence then it behooves me to continually be aware of what my attitude is really like.

A few years ago I completed a 360-degree leadership review where my peers, those I lead, my leaders and others from outside the church were invited to comment on me. The test had a boatload of questions plus some specific ones at the end.

You are measured on a range of different aspects but the toughest part was reading the answers. Despite my best efforts to work it out, you don't know who is answering – but that's not the point I want to make. The difficulty was my attitude towards the answers. Opposite answers to the same question make you question yourself and wonder which one you are. In reality, you are both. The process taught me many things and I did change how I approached some of my work and it affected my attitude as well. I made a decision that day that however hard it may be, I will never stop checking my attitude.

to my 19-year-old self:

" Come on, buck your ideas up. This is about more than image. Looking cool is one thing. Attitude is everything. The real you will eventually show up. Any pretence will be seen through by those you are leading. You can't fake it so determine to always have the best of attitudes. **"**

questions:

Let's take some time to be honest – how's your attitude? Good, bad or ugly?

What would you add to help people get their attitude right?

people want a leader they can trust

It has been a continuous discovery over the past twenty-five years of leadership that all of these layers I have been mentioning are connected. Break one, go without one, decide to have a day off from one and you potentially disconnect them all. There is a danger our leadership will begin to unravel.

Discretion. Integrity. Attitude. They all add to the level of trust-worthiness people feel you bring. There is a simple truth as a leader: **if people don't trust you, they won't**

follow you.

I have built up trust with people and then knocked it down myself. I don't need the devil to get in the way of my progress; I am perfectly capable of hijacking it all on my own. I have had golden moments of inspiration that have shown those I lead how valuable they are, followed by moments of absolute stupidity which probably had them wondering if I knew they even existed.

No one wants to think some people don't trust them. As we are learning, the best response is to do our very best in proving to them it was a genuine mistake, not deliberate, and the intention was never to cause them distress or any other negative outcome. And that's tough for any leader when you have to make decisions which impact other people's lives.

One verse which sticks with me in regards to trust is found in 1 Timothy 3 where it says, 'The overseer is to be above reproach.' It is a great place to start when it comes to leadership and trust, something I often quote when with young leaders.

Here are five things that I have learned which I believe can help build this layer of trust . . .

1. Think before you speak
In a world of immediate connection, a pause before we respond can be an invaluable tool. Fools rush in. Wait a

moment. Think it through. Gather the facts. See the whole picture. Don't just say something because you have the right; instead learn to say the right thing, at the right time. Learn how sometimes the right thing to say is nothing. *[Maybe re-read the layer about discretion.]*

2. Respect those you lead

As leaders we won't always get the opportunity to work with our friends. We have to learn to work with those we don't know as well, or maybe even struggle to get along with. Learn to respect others. The work they do. The skills they bring. The results they contribute towards. The opinions they may have. The ideas they share. To respect another is a choice. It builds trust, whereas disrespect does not. People don't follow a leader who they feel disrespected by.

3. Understand what's going on

I have made this mistake before, not really knowing what's going on with my team or with the project the team have responsibility for. Good leaders have their finger on the pulse. Leadership awareness is a necessary skill, not only in relation to your team, but also with regard to your own leadership. Know what's happening.

4. Stay secure

Nothing loses trust like an insecure leader. It can create indecision. It can weaken your leadership position. It's not about faking it but it is about understanding that we cannot reveal our insecurities to everyone all the time. Have someone you can turn to when it comes to sharing your frustrations. I have found it be true that when I think before I speak, respect those I lead and know what's going on, I don't need to feel insecure. I'm being the best leader I can be anyway.

5. Time and trust always go together

Twenty-five years of leadership doesn't come in a year. Often we are in such a hurry to be liked and believed in that we forget building trust takes time. After more than twenty years in my current church I'm hopeful I have enough in the 'trust bank' that even if I made a mistake it wouldn't be fatal to my leadership. You can't hide from the fact – trust takes time.

to my 19 year old self:

" You are very young so why should anyone trust you? What are you doing to prove to those around you that you can be trusted? Be above reproach. It's not about being perfect but it is about doing things well. **"**

questions:

What would you add to help us build our layer of trust?

How good is the account in your 'trust bank'?

19.18 Credibility

leaders must be credible

Anyone can have credibility for a moment. Do something well, experience a success, achieve a goal, reach a target – you gain a certain amount of credibility each time.

The challenge is maintaining your credibility over the long term and that can be tricky because you don't know how long that will be. Is it six months, a year, five years, a lifetime? My answer is YES. All of them.

See, my experience is this: if I want credibility then always do things well, always use discretion, always maintain and repair my integrity, always watch my attitude, always be someone others can trust. Once, though, is never really going to be enough.

For me, credibility has two levels: personal and positional.

After twenty-five years of leadership my hope is that I have earned enough credibility so when I mess up it won't be fatal to my leadership.

However, in that twenty-five years, I think I've noticed something about credibility, about how my reputation is affected by both the good and the not so good things I have done. This might take some understanding but the two are not separate, rather very much linked together.

My personal credibility can protect my positional credibility

Within reason anyway. I think if I murdered someone or committed adultery both would be affected quite seriously. However, I can look back on my life and see mistakes made but, before great damage to me and my leadership could be done, friends rallied around me, supported me, encouraged me, protected me and my reputation. They helped me journey through it. Helped me to make good decisions and stay on track. Maybe the credibility I had earned personally with them over a period of time was enough for them to think, *'this is not the real Julian here'*.

Of course, the contrary can also be true. When we don't know a person except for the position they hold, we can be quick to judge them, to almost encourage their downfall. Our assumption that somehow they should be perfect is unfair. They are only people like ourselves. Think, for example, of leaders within society, business or government. One mistake and we quickly question their reputation. We must fight against this tendency, especially those of us who are Christian leaders.

Personal credibility and positional credibility are not separate

Instead, I have realised they are inter-connected. One influences the other. Both must be protected. Yes, achieve great things. Yes, be successful. But, alongside those, build great friendships, encourage healthy relationships. Then, if/when you mess up, your personal credibility may just be enough to outweigh the damage to your positional credibility. Those closest to you can help you maintain the credibility you have worked so hard to build.

One thing is for sure, we don't know what our credibility is actually worth until we do something that makes others question it. By then it might be too late to discover if the only credibility we have is because of the position or title we possessed rather than on a personal level.

I rescued my credibility after I messed up. It was an uncomfortable time but worth the short-term pain. I had to lose the reputation I thought I had, to rebuild the one

I really needed.

When we sense we are losing our credibility, we must take responsibility for it, and not blame others. We have to work hard, put high levels of energy into making things right between us and those on our teams. We will need to admit our mistake, apologise, set things straight, make any appropriate restitution, seek reconciliation if necessary and begin to build that credibility all over again.

to my 19-year-old self:

" You may dream of being incredible but, in reality, credibility is not about fame and fortune. It's possibly more about who you are than what you do. Being credible is about being believable, so watch it. If you lack credibility it means people don't believe you. Be aware of this and commit to build it, one day at a time. "

questions:

How is your credibility?

Are there people you need to make things right with?

good leaders are reliable leaders

How do we want to be known? What words and phrases would we like people to use when speaking about us and our leadership?

If I was to ask my nineteen-year-old self how I would like to be described in the future, maybe I would have talked about being known, being successful, being recognised, being unique, being an original, maybe even being famous.

I certainly would not have chosen the word 'reliable' which

is probably one of the words people use today to describe me. Who wants to be known as reliable? How boring? Original, maverick, edgy, they sound so much more exciting.

In twenty-five years of learning, one key lesson has been that, despite the levels of charisma, talent or originality we may have as a leader, to stand the test of time reliability always wins over everything else.

People want reliability not just creativity and they want reliability because of what it represents. We may think it's a boring word yet, in actual fact, through our reliability is where all the fun, power and opportunities can be discovered. **Anyone can be creative but not everyone can demonstrate reliability.**

Like all the other layers, to be spoken of as reliable takes time, there is not a quick journey to being known as the dependable one.

How have I become reliable? Time. When others fell away or left, I have kept to the principle which was first seen in me when I was nineteen: a willingness to muck in, do whatever needs to be done, to lead from 'behind' and work on bringing the best out of others who can help.

These five things sum up the ways anyone can improve their reliability . . .

Get stuff done

There is no getting away from it, leaders get things done. They execute tasks. They can get teams working together to accomplish the great and small alike. Stop chasing the new shiny thing. Knuckle down. Complete the project.

Be known as a leader who does what they say they will do and you become known as reliable.

Keep your word

It will happen but know that no one likes a leader who is more 'do as I say' rather than 'do as I do'. If you make a commitment, keep it. If you say you will follow it up, then follow it up.

Be known as a leader who keeps their word and you become known as reliable.

Don't pass the blame

There have been a few common themes throughout these pages, one being: admit your mistakes. Take the hit. If it was your fault don't pass it over. Great leaders praise the team when it goes well and take responsibility when things fall apart.

Be known as a leader who is willing to take the blame when things go wrong and you become known as reliable.

Show up

Leaders are visible, they have a presence. Not in a bossy

or 'I have arrived' way. Instead they are involved, helping, serving, even when it's not their department's event. Leaders have given up their right to have things their own way, to not bother or be absent.

Be known as a leader who shows up with the right attitude and you become known as reliable.

Take the responsibility of leadership seriously

Reliable leaders care, they see the role as extremely important. Blasé leaders are seen as careless and lacking in dependability. Serious doesn't mean no fun, it just means you see what you do as significant and you want to do it right and with excellence.

Be known as a leader who takes their role seriously and you become known as reliable.

To be completely honest, although reliable is quite possibly one of the most boring words you can use to describe someone, I have come to appreciate and recognise its value and significance. I would rather wear this badge every day above any other name people could decide to call me.

to my 19-year-old self:

" This may not bother you now but for a lifetime journey in leadership you will learn to appreciate it. So, don't worry about becoming known as reliable. It means you have done well over the long haul and the world needs leaders who can do well and be reliable over the long haul. *"*

questions:

Who are the reliable leaders in your world?

What can you learn from watching them?

19.20 Ownership

leaders own it and help others to own it too

This one final leadership layer cannot be overlooked. To have ownership means as leaders we own it – not rocket science there. When you own something, though, you act in a different way towards it.

▌ You take care of it.

▌ You protect it.

▌ You make sure it doesn't break.

▌ If it breaks you mend it or make arrangements to have it fixed.

▌ Maybe if it's become out of date, you replace it for a newer one.

▌ You spend time, energy and money on it.

When I got given my first leadership position, I owned it. There was a team but this was my baby. I spent hours planning the sessions for each time the youth group met. I was the one who worried if it was any good or just a load of rubbish.

Even now I carry that same attitude towards the things I get to do. Whether it's as simple as putting chairs out or bringing a message on a Sunday. I own it. I do it well. I give my very best to it. Not only for my sake but more so for the sake of the recipients of what I am doing.

What I have written above is true: I did own it, it was my baby and I worked hard. At the same time as saying I owned it I also dropped the ball and demonstrated ways which have made people think I wasn't truly owning it. This can seem confusing but it's not really.

I loved taking credit when an event was successful, otherwise it was the other person's fault. I could be a good finger-pointer. Passing the buck – it's not my fault, I don't have the right resources – or other lame excuses. All just to save face.

This is why ownership is such an important aspect of leadership. We can own none, part or all of something. We can look like we own it, that we care but in reality we don't or would be happier if we didn't.

To become a good leader means this layer of leadership has to be handled carefully. After all, who wants to follow a leader who doesn't demonstrate a willingness to own what they lead (by which I mean both the task and the team of people bringing the task into reality)?

So, here are a few things I have learned along the way ...

▌ Ownership is 24/7. You either own it or you don't.

▌ Ownership is action more than words. The proof of the ownership pudding is in the eating.

▌ Ownership is about adding value wherever you can. Always bring your 'A' game.

▌ Ownership is inconvenient because it never switches off.

▌ Ownership should produce a determination to want to get it right. Not perfection but done with excellence.

▌ Ownership is for everyone. Yes, everyone.

▌ Ownership isn't easy. Why not? Just read these again.

▌ Ownership can inspire others to be involved in what you are doing. Your heart for what you are doing is a very attractive quality, even when what you are doing is not particularly attractive.

▌ Ownership shows how much you care. Otherwise you wouldn't really be owning it, you'd just be faking it.

▌ Ownership is always in the context of the bigger picture. Learn to see how what you do fits in to the overall vision. Most times, what you own wouldn't exist if it wasn't for the bigger vision.

Don't step up if you are unwilling to grasp full responsibility for what you are taking ownership of. If you don't own it, you will not get given it.

Or, if in your leadership position you demonstrate a lack of ownership, be prepared that it may well be taken out of your hands.

to my 19-year-old self:

" Pick up the ball, run with it, take hold of some responsibility, get involved, have a go. Own it. Make something happen. And whatever the pressure, the response from others, the lack of appreciation, don't just let go, drop the ball or display an attitude of 'I don't care'. "

questions:

Think of what you are leading. How are you demonstrating ownership?

How will you improve the way you own what you are leading?

19.21 Self-Awareness

leaders know themselves well

As someone starting out in leadership, let me ask you a question: how's your self-awareness?

It is more acceptable nowadays to reflect, to have a coach or mentor, to be accountable. Leadership has become an industry all of its own. Add to this a whole library of self-help and improvement books and there is less of an excuse to not have some degree of self-awareness.

In my twenty-five years of leadership I have learned the

need to stand in front of the leadership mirror and give myself an honest once-over and increase my leadership self-awareness. This is not a one-time exercise either.

A look in the leadership mirror of self-awareness can help you recognise things about yourself and the way that you lead. For want of a better way to describe what I mean, sometimes it's been an **UGLY** view:

*U*nderstanding two things: who you are and who you are not

This is a very important aspect of leadership. 'This is me, get over it', rarely works for leaders. It's a bit ignorant really and not many people want to follow an ignorant leader. If you don't know yourself well it doesn't breed confidence in the team that you know them.

The 360-degree leadership review I mentioned previously was part of discovering who I was and who I was not. Maybe do a personality test or a Spiritual Gift finder to help know about what makes you tick. Then you can find your right fit, which will in turn help you to help others find their right fit.

On too many occasions I have shown a complete lack of understanding. I have pushed too hard. I have ignored feelings and emotions. I have disrespected people's circumstances and lives. I have not taken the time to know them and find how to get the best out of them. I have used 'the way I am' as a convenient get-out clause. That

leaders know themselves well

is WRONG.

Gracious enough to realise two things: you are not as good as your best day or as bad as your worst

A smug leader is an ugly leader. To be gracious is to be humble and to acknowledge the role that the whole team plays in any success.

Let me give you an example. One of the things we did back in the church in Sheffield was a youth drop-in on a Thursday night. It was an incredible night, beyond expectations, with over two hundred young people turning up. A 'best day'.

The next day there was a phone call from the minister and a conversation about broken toilets, lots of mess and although there was recognition for success in one aspect with the numbers, the damage very quickly become the focus. A 'worst' day.

I like to do well. When I was younger my drive to win would make me an ungracious team player, especially when others let me down. Age, experience and a willingness to adjust have brought some good changes during the past twenty-five years as a leader. Don't get me wrong, I'm still competitive, just a better winner and loser. Add to that my philosophy of being willing to be doing whatever needs to be done – and I truly mean 'whatever'.

Learning that leadership is about two things: what you do and, more importantly, why you do it

We may tick the box of doing but what are we learning about ourselves on the way?

I am very determined in my desire to learn, not just techniques and ideas but about myself. I have developed some ways to help me learn all the time. Great leaders are continuously checking themselves. They are observing not just what they do, but the motives and thoughts behind why they are doing that particular thing.

I can be my own worst critic. Did I do enough? Have I planned adequately? Have I helped the team succeed? What could I have done differently? Thankfully, over the years this has shifted from reasons of selfish ambition to the desire just to be the best version of me I can be.

You need two things: the divine grace of God and people

I am conscious that when it comes to fulfilling the leadership role I am in now, it is not about me. I am not qualified for the position. I am unable to accomplish the role on my own.

As a Christian leader I need two things which can help me in my daily decisions and in overcoming my mistakes: I need the divine grace of God and I need people. God at the centre of all I do, and a great team to do life with every day. I am thankful that I have both.

However, it is easy to get these the wrong way around and, as a lover of good systems and process, it can happen too easily. The practical can often take precedence over the presence. As much as we need both, the presence and the practical, it is vital to make sure we don't swap the presence of God for the practical in terms of importance. Without the presence of God we may find ourselves working out of our own strength.

From age nineteen to today I am discovering that a little **UGLY** leadership is actually a good thing.

Understanding two things: who you are and who you are not.

Gracious enough to realise two things: you are not as good as your best day or as bad as your worst.

Learning that leadership is about two things: what you do and, more importantly, why you do it.

You need two things: the divine grace of God and people.

to my 19-year-old self:

" You live with you all the time, so get to know yourself better. What do you love to do? What stirs your heart? Ask God to move in your life and reveal stuff which needs dealing with all with the purpose of being the best version of you and available for God to use. **"**

question:

What have you learned so far about yourself on your leadership journey?

19.22 Coming Under

the best leaders are willing to come under the authority of their own leaders

'I want to do what I want to do.' Sounds fair, although a bit childish too. 'Don't you know who I am? I'm the leader.'

[Pause]

As you have discovered, my journey as a leader has taught me many things and one of the tougher lessons has been this: *'It's not about me.'* As always, with any lesson which has to be learned, it's very easy to say but harder sometimes to believe.

If we cannot learn to come under authority we will struggle to be someone in authority

'I'm in charge' is having authority but doesn't necessarily make you a leader people want to listen to or follow.

My own personal experience of thinking I can do what I like and still be a great leader brought about lessons I definitely learned the hard way. I perhaps thought I was untouchable, invincible maybe. God's grace is amazing that you can have such a stinking attitude, make some really dubious lifestyle decisions yet He still makes incredible things happen and young people's lives are changed. However, it doesn't make those 'things' any less wrong.

I have spoken before about being called to account for actions, challenged on my attitude and how I was living. Tough, uncomfortable conversations are all a part of the process of learning to come under the authority of others.

Learning to respect those in positions of spiritual authority is difficult, especially if you don't like hearing what they are saying. Look for the fruit they produce.

Check their hearts. They are human, after all, and will most certainly get it wrong at times but so do we. Yet submission to those in spiritual authority over our lives brings more benefits than concerns.

I have benefited from coming under authority more than I have ever felt constrained by it

Coming under has brought me freedom to become who God wanted me to become, with boundaries that afforded me the protection I needed when I didn't even realise I needed it.

Although the vision I have for what I am leading or want to lead may be amazing, it remains irrelevant if I haven't considered the bigger vision it is a part of. After all, without the bigger vision of the church, the ministry I lead would not exist. They have to stay connected and by coming under I am honouring the vision of my leader.

Coming under authority has kept me safe in my leadership

Yes, it brings accountability, but it also brings so much more. Spiritual authority over my life is about leaders praying for me, speaking into my life, encouraging me and walking alongside me.

The alternative to coming under authority would have been me being my own authority and making my own decisions. One without consultation of others who could have offered wisdom, insight, clarity and better ideas to undoubtedly bring about an end game including less upset and regret for me and for others, too. I may have also thought that the grass was greener somewhere else when it really wasn't.

Now I have the privilege and responsibility of being one of those who is in a position of spiritual authority. To stand up for those following me. To pray for them. To assist them. To cover them and, at times, cover for them. To help them see beyond what is just in front and have an eye for the bigger picture they are part of. To help them hear what God is saying for them and their future.

It's never been about me and it never will be. My heart has always been focused on ensuring I am positioned right as a Christian leader so I don't make any stupid mistakes and disqualify myself from what God has for me to do.

Thank you to those who watched out for me in the past. Without such cover I may not be where I am today, doing what I am doing, with my beautiful family and the incredible people I get to do life with every day.

to my 19-year-old self:

" I acknowledge this isn't always easy, after all we like our independence. BUT be willing to listen to your leaders. Come under the protection and guidance of their leadership and spiritual authority. I am certain I would not be doing what I am doing today if I had chosen to go my own way. **"**

question:

Why might you struggle to come under another person's leadership?

Go and see your leaders. Be specific about telling them thank you for their leadership and to ask them to continue to speak into your life.

part three: now

know that greater awaits

Back in 1989 greatness looked similar but different to how greatness appears today. Fame was still fame; the main difference was you actually had to be doing something to achieve fame. It just seems like it was about more than being able to sing badly, or live in a house for so many weeks, or appear in any other reality TV show.

Greatness as a leader in the mind of a 'cool' nineteen-year-old may have included such things as their name in lights or being recognised as one of the all-time greats in a particular field of expertise. Yet greatness in leadership from God's perspective can be very different.

You learn these truths as you stay on the journey. Mostly because the greatness we may look for from the world's perspective is still hard to accomplish.

We are possibly one step away from greatness. One step away from being incredible for God.

Or maybe we are one step away from a great act of stupidity. One step away from making ourselves invisible for God.

We have to learn to recognise that God's way to greatness may be different to ours. He uses every experience to shape us for our future. Greater awaits.

Joseph dreamt of greatness (Genesis 37). Like most seventeen-year-olds he could not have imagined the journey he would travel to achieve such greatness. He discovered greatness with God is upside down to that of the world.

▌ Greatness was about fame, but not Joseph's.

▌ Greatness was about building something of worth, but not for Joseph.

▌ Greatness was about success, but not based on the currency of the current culture.

▌ Greatness was about winning, but not at the expense of everyone else losing.

Now I know, to be a great leader for God He views it in a different way. When I was younger I was waiting for my 'moment'.

▌ Greatness with God is not a moment, a one hit wonder, it's not our fifteen minutes of fame, or to make a million or two.

God is not shaping me or wanting me to be ready for a moment like this, instead He is looking for me and for leaders who are ready for **any moment.** Moments that come when you're not expecting them. Moments that are not epic but demonstrate a heart and life dedicated to serving God.

▌ **Any moment** of greatness comes by walking with God and doing what He is asking you to do and continuing to do so every day.

▌ **Any moment** of greatness comes by serving others first, not looking for others to serve you.

▌ **Any moment** of greatness comes by sacrificing time, talent and resource to make God famous.

▌ **Any moment** of greatness comes by displaying loyalty, resisting temptation, working hard, noticing the sadness of the faces of those around you, ministering to others, hearing from God, handling adversity, handling promotion, forgiving, and seeing God's hand over your life.

Let's stop waiting for 'the' moment and instead be ready

for 'any' moment and see all the great things God has for us to do throughout all of our life.

Not all time in life is equal. Life serves up some moments that count much more than other moments. Some moments are more important than others. They have the potential to define us. Will we be ready?

We determine whether the moment will pull us ahead, cause us to fall behind or kill us off.

So here goes. Here is how to be better prepared for the greater things God has for us. Will we be prayed up and confident enough in the Word of God that when the moment comes we won't miss it?

Here's the thing. We mustn't wait for the opportunity to come before getting prepared. At that moment it's often too late. Start preparations today in two vital areas . . .

Your prayer life
It will define you. If you are not in conversation with God then you may miss it.

Your reading of the Word of God
It will shape you. Knowing He has created you for more and understanding better how God sees you will ready you for when any moment comes.

Our future awaits us. It won't arrive easily. There will be

challenges. There will be some obstacles. There will be times of defeat. There will be times of victory. Prayer and the Word will help you to navigate these times and to see you through to the other side. It might look different to what you thought it would but you know without doubt it's where God has taken you.

You don't realise this at the start. I didn't. Back then it was about surviving, getting over the nerves, and what I will get to do. Yet the longer you travel the leadership journey the more you appreciate how the destination will never be reached. Every success, mistake, opportunity and experience is merely an addition to the layers of leadership required for all that God has for you to do next.

to my 19-year-old self:

" Get ready. Greatness awaits. But you're probably going to have to wait for it. God is never in a hurry. In the meantime, do your very best when any moment comes along. **"**

questions:

How does your view of greatness for God need to change?

What one thing could you do to demonstrate to God how you are a leader ready for 'any moment'?

19.24 Empowering

leaders must look to the next generation of leaders

Been thinking about this recently and how difficult I find this. I don't think I am alone in finding this essential aspect of leadership such a challenge. All leaders know that empowering others is the only way to bring about all that we want to see.

Doesn't make it easy though.

Empowering is about making space for people of all ages but especially the next generation. It's about releasing people and providing them with opportunities to put their gifts and talents to use.

Ultimately empowering can be us getting out of the way so others can learn and therein is the reason why it can be so difficult. Here are some quick thoughts as to why we don't get out of the way and reasons why we should.

Why we don't . . .

I **We like control.** We like to be in charge, to know what's going on.

I **We don't trust others.** No one can do it like we do it.

I **There isn't anyone to 'get out of the way' for.** Or at least that's what we convince ourselves.

I **We are scared of change.** They will do it differently to how we have done it.

I **We will have nothing to do.** We could become outdated, unwanted, or redundant.

I **What if they get it wrong**. It's just not worth the risk.

I **What if they get it right.** What we were doing might come in to question.

Why we should . . .

I **We won't achieve the vision without them.** The

bigger the vision the more we need others to help us. One person can only do so much.

▌ ***We stifle growth.*** Other people's, maybe even our own, too, and definitely the organisation's.

▌ ***We have to be willing to challenge the process.*** Just because it's always been done 'that way' doesn't mean it should continue to be. Sometimes we need that 'upstart' to say, 'Why not?'

▌ ***New people usually bring fresh energy.*** This keeps bringing that much needed life to wherever you are leading.

▌ ***They may leave if we don't.*** If people want to help but cannot see that they will ever be included, then they will probably go to a place where that does happen.

How we should do it . . .

▌ ***On purpose not haphazardly.*** Have a plan on how responsibility will be given. Create a programme maybe with a clear pathway and what those who are getting involved can expect.

▌ ***Through coaching and not just through teaching.*** You can't really 'have a go' without being given the opportunity to 'have a go'. Hands-on experience alongside some teaching can work really well. John C. Maxwell would teach us: ' a leader knows the way, goes the way, and shows the way'. Or, in other words, 'monkey see, monkey do'.

▌ ***By letting go.*** The first time is the hardest but if you have invested well then it's not the challenge you really fear.

▍ **Be an inspiring leader.** Spend your leadership being the kind of leader that others would want to be like. Inspire with vision, with attitude, with integrity, with your work ethic, with communication, with encouragement and every facet of your leadership.

▍ **Resource them.** Just keep passing on everything you know, everything you have learned. Talk all the time about the why behind what you have asked them to do.

It's a challenge but the rewards mean all that we are building can outlast us. If we make it all about us then what we are doing may well die when we die. If we make it about others then what we are building can last for generations to come.

to my 19-year-old self:

// Hope you are catching my heart. My prayer for you is that you are still leading in twenty-five years. Invest in yourself so you can start investing in others. You are never too young to take what you are learning and to pass it on. **//**

questions:

Is there anything you would add to this list?

Make a list of key things you have learned.

Make a list of three or four people who you could now coach with what you have learned.

Carry On

leaders keep leading

'I've started, so I'll finish'

You may not recognise these words as the famous line from the programme *Mastermind*. When the buzzer went off halfway through a question being asked, Magnus Magnusson (the original host of the show) would always say to them, 'I've started, so I'll finish.'

Those five words could describe what it means to be a leader. Well, at least someone who wants to be a leader for the long haul.

John C. Maxwell tells us that for leaders to go up, they have to give up. We give up our rights as we take on greater responsibility.

In simple terms, we can no longer be 'not bothered'. As a senior leader in my local church I have, over time, willingly given up my right to have a Sunday off. I can't just choose to not be there. I am, after all, one of the Pastors.

This is not the same for everyone else. Those who are not helping to make church happen, except through their attendance, have all the rights. They have the right to come, to not come, to stay at home, to give it a miss.

Think about it: if your leader started being absent, you might wonder what on earth is going on. The occasional miss could be acceptable in the short term but when they are never about it signals only one thing: the beginning of the end of their leadership.

Leaders are present

This is not necessarily about asserting our 'in-chargeness' but more about being seen encouraging and applauding people doing the right things.

Leaders lead

All that we have discussed in this book – that is what leaders do, continuously.

Leaders show up
Even when it's not 'their' event or ministry, they are there to lend support to others.

Leaders help create the right atmosphere
We bring life, energy and passion. This is not about being loud or jumping up and down. This is about believing in what you are building, and for me as a Christian leader, who I am building for.

Leaders take full responsibility
We are the ones who have stepped up and stepped in. We may delegate some stuff and have a team around us but, ultimately, the responsibility is on us.

So you have started leading, my best advice now is this . . .

▌ Keep going, keep showing up, keep leading, keep giving it your best, keep learning, keep serving, keep staying close to God.

▌ Don't quit when it gets tough.

▌ Don't disappear when challenges come your way, which they will.

▌ Don't leave your position unless it's absolutely appropriate for you to do so.

▌ Don't do something daft which could compromise your influence. But if you do, make it right as quickly as you can.

Simple. Easy. You can do it. I believe in you. And more importantly, so does God.

Somehow I have come out the other side. 'I made it!' From a lanky nineteen-year-old to an enigmatic forty-something-year-old (my description). Time has gone by so fast. And it will for you, too.

To my 19 year old self:

" Carry on leading. Set your heart towards being the best you can be, not for yourself but for your Saviour who you represent. Get set for the future and still being around. Make it known to God that you are open and available. Ask Him to use you however and I guarantee, He will. **"**

notes

19.0
'Leadership is a journey, not a destination.' This is part of a quote attributed to John Donahoe, then President of eBay.

19.1
'Leaders give up to go up': Maxwell, John C., 'The Law of Sacrifice', *The 21 Irrefutable Laws of Leadership*, (Thomas Nelson, 2007).

19.2.3
Quote attributed to Giuseppe Tomasi di Lampedusa (23 December 1896 to 26 July 1957), who was an Italian writer and the last Prince of Lampedusa. He is most famous for his only novel, *Il Gattopardo* (first published posthumously in 1958, translated as *The Leopard*).

19.5

'Leaders are readers' is part of a fuller quote attributed to Harry S. Truman: 'Not all readers are leaders, but all leaders are readers.'

19.5

Books mentioned:

Batterson, Mark, *The Circle Maker* (Zondervan, 2012).

Belsky, Scott, *Making Ideas Happen* (Penguin Books, 2011).

Carnegie, Dale, *How to Win Friends and Influence People*, new ed. edition (Vermilion, 2006).

Chand, Samuel, *Cracking Your Church's Culture Code* (Jossey-Bass, 2010).

Collins, Jim, *Great by Choice* (Random House Business, 2011).

Gladwell, Malcolm, *Outliers* (Penguin Books, 2009).

Hybels, Bill, *Axiom* (Zondervan, 2008)

Hybels, Bill, *Courageous Leadership* (Zondervan, 2012).

Lewis, C.S., *Mere Christianity*, 50th anniversary edition (HarperCollins, 2011).

Matthesius, Jurgen, *PUSH* (Thomas Nelson, 2014).

Maxwell, John C., *Developing the Leader Within You*, revised edition (Thomas Nelson, 2012).

Maxwell, John C., *The 21 Irrefutable Laws of Leadership*, 2nd revised edition (Thomas Nelson, 2007).

Posner and Kouzes, *The Leadership Challenge*, 6th revised edition (John Wiley & Sons, 2017).

Sanders, J. Oswald, *Spiritual Leadership* (Moody Publishers, 2007).

Stanley, Andy, *The Next Generation Leader*, (Mulnomah UK, 2006).

19.8

Psalm 15, Holy Bible, New International Version (Anglicised edition). Copyright © 1979, 1984, 2011 by Biblica (formerly International Bible Society). Used by permission of Hodder & Stoughton Publishers, an Hachette UK company. All rights reserved.

Posner and Kouzes, *The Leadership Challenge*, 6th revised edition (John Wiley & Sons, 2017).

19.10

Conners, Smith, Hickman, *The Oz Principle* (Portfolio, 2011).

19.11

Maxwell, John C., 'The Law of the Lid', *The 21 Irrefutable Laws of Leadership*, 2nd revised edition (Thomas Nelson, 2007).

Proverbs 27:6, Holy Bible, New King James Version. Copyright © 1982 by Thomas Nelson. Used by permission. All rights reserved.

19.14

Definition of 'Discretion', Oxford Dictionaries (OUP).

Proverbs 2:11 (NKJV).

19.15

Cloud, Dr Henry, *Integrity: The Courage to Meet the Demands of Reality* (Harper Business, 2009),

19.17

1 Timothy 3:2, (NIV).

19.23

The story of Joseph can be found in Genesis chapters 37 – 50.

CARRY ON

'I've started so I'll finish' was a catchphrase used by Magnus Magnusson when he presented the long-running quiz show *Mastermind* from 1972 to 1997, which the current presenter John Humphrys has continued to use (Wikipedia, accessed June 2017).

about the author

Julian was given his first leadership opportunity when he was nineteen years old, at the youth group at Totley Rise Methodist Church in Sheffield, the church he attended while at University.

Now, more than twenty-five years later, he lives in the North East of England, and is married to Kerina, who he met when the youth group he led came to visit her church in Newton Aycliffe. Together they have served in a variety of leadership roles during the past twenty-four years at Xcel Church, where Julian is currently the Executive Pastor.

Julian has a heart to raise up future leaders. He has a wealth of experience in leadership development from twenty-plus years of involvement in designing leadership development programmes, regularly teaching teams, mentoring and coaching leaders in church as well as through time spent as a Learning Mentor working in local schools, colleges and universities, and being a qualified Life Coach.

Julian loves local church. He is passionate about walking with God and becoming all that God desires for him. Now, through his current role, he is in the privileged position of being able to help others discover their potential too.

Julian and Kerina live in Newton Aycliffe and have three beautiful daughters, Lucy, Maisie and Grace.

Find out more about Julian and The 19 Project, a site to help raise and resource leaders, by visiting **the19project.com**.

<u>pr</u>ayer

We hope you enjoyed this book and that it has been both a blessing and a challenge to your life and walk with God. Maybe you just got hold of it and are glancing through before starting. We made the decision as a publishing company right from the start never to take for granted that everyone has prayed a prayer to receive Jesus as their Lord, so we are including that as the finale to this book. If you have never asked Jesus into your life and would like to do that now, it's so easy. Just pray this simple prayer:

Dear Lord Jesus,
Thank You for dying on the cross for me. I
believe that You gave Your life so that I could
have life. When You died on the cross, You died
as an innocent man who had done nothing
wrong. You were paying for my sins and the
debt I could never pay. I believe in You, Jesus,

> *and receive the brand new life and fresh start*
> *that the Bible promises that I can have. Thank*
> *You for my sins forgiven, for the righteousness*
> *that comes to me as a gift from You, for hope*
> *and love beyond what I have known and the*
> *assurance of eternal life that is now mine.*
> *Amen.*

Good next moves are to get yourself a Bible that is easy to understand and begin to read. Maybe start in John so you can discover all about Jesus for yourself. Start to pray – prayer is simply talking to God – and, finally, find a church that's alive and get your life planted in it. These simple ingredients will cause your relationship with God to grow.

Why not email us and let us know if you did that so we can rejoice with you?

info@greatbiglifepublishing.com

further
information

For further information about the author of this book, or to order more copies, please contact:

Great Big Life Publishing
Empower Centre
83-87 Kingston Road
Portsmouth
Hampshire
PO2 7DX
United Kingdom
info@greatbiglifepublishing.com

are you an author?

Do you have a word from God on your heart that you'd like to get published to a wider audience? We're looking for manuscripts that identify with our own vision of bringing life-giving and relevant messages to the Body of Christ. Send yours for review towards possible publication to:

Great Big Life Publishing
Empower Centre
83-87 Kingston Road
Portsmouth
Hampshire
PO2 7DX
United Kingdom
info@greatbiglifepublishing.com